THE 10 HABITS OF
HIGHLY SUCCESSFUL
WOMEN

THE 10 HABITS OF HIGHLY SUCCESSFUL WOMEN

Edited by Glynnis MacNicol and Rachel Sklar

amazonpublishing

Published by Amazon Publishing, New York

www.apub.com

ISBN-13: 9781477819692
ISBN-10: 147781969X

Cover design by Natalia Suárez

"There's a lot of money to be made by taking women seriously."
—Cindy Gallop

CONTENTS

1. Emotional Correctness *Sally Kohn*
2. Why I Never Tell Anyone My Age *Nisha Chittal*
3. Starting from the Bottom *Jenna Wortham*
4. Will the Lady in the Bubble Please Let the Cat Out of the Bag? *Ruth Ann Harnisch*
5. Controlled Burn *Paula Froelich*
6. It Is Never Too Late to Change Everything *Leslie Bradshaw*
7. Willing to Be Lucky *Glynnis MacNicol*
8. Go Fund Yourself *Rachel Sklar*
9. A Culture of Extraordinary *Stacy London*
10. Changing the World through Business and Sex *Cindy Gallop*

1.
EMOTIONAL CORRECTNESS

Sally Kohn

Y ou know your secret weapon?" Fox News host Sean Hannity · once asked me. "You're likeable," he said, and then gave me a hug. Which might be a surprising scenario for anyone, but especially a left-leaning lesbian like me.

How did that happen? I spent the first sixteen years of my career as a community organizer, working to help ordinary people make extraordinary changes in their communities—whether fixing a broken stoplight or passing health-care reform. Then, rather suddenly, a television executive saw me speaking at a conference in 2009 and came up to me afterward and said, "We should get you on television." I demurred. She insisted. And less than a year later, after some great training and good luck, I was hired by the Fox News Channel to be an on-air commentator arguing about politics and current events from a progressive perspective.

People, mostly other liberals, always ask me what it's like to be "in the lion's den" at Fox News. I could tell them what they probably expect to hear—that everyone has fangs and is very mean. But it's not true. Sure, the hate mail is atrocious—pretty much every time I would go on air and defend some basic liberal position on an issue, whether raising the minimum wage or ensuring access to contraception for women, or even defending the basic existence of government of, for, and by the people, I would receive a trove of hate mail, not just attacking my opinions but attacking me as a person. Hate mail slathered with sexism and homophobia. I even get racist hate mail, which is saying a lot considering I'm as white as untanned snow. But the fact is, everyone in the public eye gets hate mail—and women and people of color and gay folks in the public eye, whether they're on the right or the left, get extra-ugly hate mail. Do folks on the left get it worse than folks on the right? Frankly, I don't know, and I don't care. There's a lot of nastiness spewed in all directions.

But the people at Fox News? The people I debated on air, whether Sean Hannity, Bill O'Reilly, Ann Coulter, or you name it? The folks behind the scenes, whether the head of the network or the producers and camera operators? They couldn't be more lovely. For me, who certainly walked into the building the first time with a lot of unconfessed stereotypes about conservatives, it was a stark realization about how we put each other into political boxes of "otherness" that have nothing to do with reality. Sean Hannity and I have almost nothing in common politically, but fortunately our politics are only a fraction of who we are as people. And as people, as human beings, we have a ton in common. That's not to say our political differences aren't important. I'm a political pundit. Trust me, I think those political differences are incredibly profound and vital. They're just not the sum total of what defines us.

Being face-to-face with some of the most well-known conservatives in America, and forging personal relationships with them, especially when the cameras were off, made me appreciate our commonalities far more than I'd ever before imagined. Which made me realize that I have more in common with all conservatives than I think—and that starting with those commonalities, making those connections, is the key to building relationships and therefore being persuasive. That, in a nutshell, is "emotional correctness."

Emotional correctness is *how* we say what we say—the tone and feeling we convey, the respect and empathy we show others not necessarily with our words even, but our style. After all, people won't hear anything we're saying if they don't listen to us first. And we get people to listen to us by being emotionally correct.

Emotional correctness is how we show each other that we care, on a human level, regardless of whether we agree or disagree on political, or any other, terms. There's a way to see this in purely transactional terms: It's hard enough to get audiences or employees or potential customers to listen to ideas that seem wildly different from what they've heard before. It's near impossible to get them to hear different ideas from *people* who seem wildly different—or, even more extreme, who seem dangerously different. In the small parts of our mammalian brains, we resort to our prehistoric habits of dividing everyone we encounter into friend or foe. Those we think are friends are embraced, literally and, in terms of their ideas, figuratively too. Those who are foes? That's where the fight-or-flight instinct kicks in. We either instantly start arguing with and rebutting everything they say (fight) or tune them out altogether (flight). Now, pragmatically speaking, what category do you want to be put in? Emotional correctness is how you get in the circle with your audience, connect with them as a friend not a foe, and start the conversations that lead to change.

Beyond the practical advantage of getting your audience to like you and listen to you, rather than tune you out, there's another way in which emotional correctness appeals—to the larger, philosophical ideal of a pluralistic and democratic nation in which, sure, we're all different, yet we still find ways to connect and work together.

That somewhat Pollyannaish ideal is rooted in the founding values of our nation, that our diversity of experiences and opinions makes us stronger, not weaker—that out of many we are one. Those of us who believe passionately in the American political experiment, from the highest halls of government down to each individual neighborhood and small business, know that as Abraham Lincoln once said, "a house divided against itself cannot stand." That division can come in the form of civil war or just the cultural and political divides that risk making us feel like separate nations. Finding ways to cross those divides, to unite as people even if we cannot agree on politics, is essential to our national survival.

So whether you want to engage a reticent audience to buy your product or find ways to bridge the deep schisms of political and cultural identity, emotional correctness is both a philosophy and a tool for authentically finding compassion with others and forging the sorts of connections through which real listening and persuasion are possible. In the following pages, we'll explore the science of emotional correctness—and how it can make you more persuasive and effective. And we'll explore the practice of emotional correctness—offering five strategies for dialing up emotional correctness in your life and career.

The Science of Emotional Correctness

Over two thousand years ago, Aristotle wrote that persuasion is dependent on the character of the person doing the persuading. This has been confirmed by decades and decades of social-science research since. My favorite study was conducted in 1979 by Shelly Chaiken. Chaiken recruited 110 University of Massachusetts undergraduates to stop passersby along the university lawn and deliver a persuasive message about how the school should stop serving meat in campus cafeterias—a fairly controversial message for the late 1970s. What did Chaiken find? That the students who were most persuasive had one thing in common—they were also the most attractive.

No, the key to emotional correctness isn't smoldering eyes or even plastic surgery. Though smoldering eyes can't hurt. What Chaiken's study reinforces is the fundamental principle that attraction is one way we decide whether we like someone, and likeability is a fundamental part of persuasion. Emotional correctness is about making authentic, heartfelt connections with people—and when people make those connections with us, we tend to like them more.

Tracing the word *like* back to its roots in Old English as well as Dutch and German, it actually means "of the same body." Liking someone, or feeling that you are like someone, is literally like closing the physical and conceptual distance between you and the other person, connecting to your mutual sameness. Which suggests, incidentally, that Chaiken's study said more about the subjects than the interviewers—that we are more persuaded by attractive messengers because we like to think of ourselves as attractive.

By the same token, the word *persuasion* derives from the root *swad* meaning sweet. There's even some evidence tying the word *persuasion* to Suada who was the Roman goddess who attended to Venus, the goddess of love. Basically, emotional correctness just makes us feel all yummy and sexy and good—and we like listening when we feel liked or even loved. Historically, scientists and philosophers called this the law of affinity.

Dr. Karen Stephenson is a corporate anthropologist, a term that makes me picture Dilbert wearing war paint. The law of affinity, says Stephenson is "an ancient skill encoded in us by our forebears."[1] We human beings need each other emotionally, and there's safety in numbers physically. So we're inclined to bond together intellectually, to mold our opinions to the group, out of our desire to belong.

That's right—emotional correctness breeds affinity, which makes us more inclined to mold our opinions to match those of the person we like, or at least be open to them. Seem too simple? Meet Joe Girard.

Almost thirty-five years after his retirement, Joe Girard still holds the record as the World's Greatest Salesman. As a car and truck dealer from 1963 to 1978, Girard personally sold over 13,000 vehicles. Actually, 13,001 to be exact. In his best year, 1973, Girard sold an average of four-and-a-half cars a day if you don't count Sundays. Joe Girard is a damn good salesman.

So what's his trick? Every month, Joe sent a letter to every one of the 13,000 customers on his mailing list. And it said, simply, "I like you." If the letter came around a holiday, it might say, "I like you. Happy Thanksgiving!" But every letter always said pretty much the same thing: I like you. Every month. By hand. Mailed to 13,000 people. Way before e-mail.

When people walked into his showroom, Girard handed them a pin that said—you guessed it—"I like you." Girard explained, "Even if you don't buy, I like you . . . but I know you will buy." And in a sign that Girard evolved with the times, he even has "I like you!" included in his Twitter bio. Emotional correctness—being likeable, projecting kindness and connection toward others—was the key to Joe Girard's success.

In one social-science study, researchers would ask subjects for a favor—but would first make various comments to the subjects, either compliments, criticisms, or some mix. No big surprise that when the researcher gave positive comments, he was liked the most by subjects. But get this—the likeability effect stayed the same whether the compliments were true or false.[2] The subjects just liked feeling liked. And in the study, flattery made the subjects more likely to perform the requested favor.

Emotional correctness makes people respond more positively toward you because people respond positively in general when they feel positive—and emotional correctness is about building that kind, warm, compassionate connection. Arguably, the effect is even greater when emotional correctness is authentic, not something you conjure up for expedience or a research study.

In 2004, three years after he left the White House, Bill Clinton was interviewed by Oprah Winfrey for *O, The Oprah Magazine*. "Why do black people like you so much?" Winfrey asked.

"We like people who like us. They like me 'cause I like them and they know it," said Clinton.[3] And we all know Bill Clinton can teach a master class on emotional correctness.

Likeability is the most studied manifestation of emotional correctness, but likeability by itself is complicated. Facebook COO Sheryl Sandberg has spoken about the "likeability trade-off" that women face—that the more successful women become, the less likeable they are in the eyes of others. That is messed up. And it suggests that women and, arguably, people of color and gay folks and others face a zero-sum choice. The fact is that it's hard for a gay man of color who pops up in front of a conservative audience to reap the "he's just like me" benefit of the doubt that the same audience may readily give someone else. The choice, then, is to either screw emotional correctness and settle for being righteous but marginalized—an understandable choice that many a cruel boss and isolated ideologue have made—or, we can consciously dial up our emotional correctness even more, knowing that it may be unfair, but it's also necessary.

In an article for the *Harvard Business Review*, John Neffinger, Matt Kohut, and Amy Cuddy write:

> A growing body of research suggests that the way to influence—and to lead—is to begin with warmth. Warmth is the conduit of influence: It facilitates trust and the communication and absorption of ideas. Even a few small nonverbal signals—a nod, a smile, an open gesture—can

show people that you're pleased to be in their company and attentive to their concerns. Prioritizing warmth helps you connect immediately with those around you, demonstrating that you hear them, understand them, and can be trusted by them.[4]

Their article is titled, "Connect, Then Lead." Connection comes through emotional correctness.

In 1950, the literary theorist Kenneth Burke wrote *A Rhetoric of Motives*, a groundbreaking text on how rhetoric is used to persuade—which, after all, is really why we try to connect with people at all, whether our goal is to persuade someone to change her or his mind about a political issue or buy a product or get them into bed. Burke posited that all persuasion is rooted in identification—the idea that for persuasion to occur, you have to "identify" with or decide you're like the person doing the persuading.

For Burke, this was ultimately the root of all social cohesion. For me, not writing off half of the population as politically or socially alien, but actively trying to persuade others through connection—through emotional correctness—may be the way of getting some of that social cohesion back.

The Practice of Emotional Correctness

There is clearly a moral and psychological imperative behind emotional correctness. It works to make you more persuasive but, as or arguably even more important, it also makes you more human. I write this as a total political animal, yet I still dream of a day when we can be human beings first and political beings second. Or human beings first and bosses and employees second. Or what have you. I'm not saying we all have to hold hands and sing "Kumbaya." Please, no. But I am saying we can do ourselves and our society a great service—and be more effective and heard—by authentically, empathetically connecting with one another. Which sounds really good in theory. Here's how you do it in practice.

Picture your aunt as your audience. I have an aunt. Several of them, actually, but one in particular who I picture when I'm talking to most any audience but especially a group that isn't filled with rabid left-wing partisans like me. I'm not going to give you the details about my aunt, because if you start picturing her, you might deplete her magical powers in my own concocted scenarios . . . but suffice it to say, she's a middle-of-the-road-leaning-conservative, loving Midwestern mom and grandma who might not agree with me on most issues but is certainly a kind and decent person and will always disagree with a big smile on her face.

If I'm debating some Tea Party personality on television, it's easy to imagine that person is my audience—and try to shape my arguments to win him over. News flash: I can't. That person I'm arguing with is as committed to his or her views as I am—otherwise neither of us would be on television. We'd be off somewhere still figuring out what we think. But more importantly, who cares. Persuading my opponent on air isn't the point. My goal is to influence and persuade the millions of people watching at home, people like my aunt. So I picture her and talk to her—not to my cardboard foil.

Sometimes you have your real audience in front of you—at a speech or in a classroom or at a product pitch. But even then, it can be hard to really know who they are—and remember the ways in which they're different from you and, therefore, the gaps you need to bridge in order to make connections. If you can grab hold of a mental archetype, ideally an image of a real person like my aunt, then you can concretely imagine what that person is thinking and feeling and doubting and fearing, and you can connect with those emotional needs.

Smile and your audience will smile with you. Picturing someone you know and love as your target audience also helps with a big piece of emotional correctness—smiling. Like I said, my aunt may not always agree with me, but she at least does it with a smile. And I smile right back. What kind of a loving niece would I be if I didn't? This is kind of a no-brainer when you think about it, but it is nonetheless hard to remember in the moment—if you want people to think you're likeable, then you need to look likeable. And the biggest way to signal that is with a warm and genuine smile.

People can tell when you're faking it. Scientists have a name for that—the "polite" smile, as opposed to the full-face "genuine smile," where the muscles around your eyes are engaged, and the corners crinkle up toward your eyebrows.[5] In one study, subjects were matched up to play a game to try to win money against computer-generated opponents who either had polite smiles or genuine smiles during the game. Afterward, subjects were asked which "opponents" they preferred playing with. The deciding factor? Turns out the subjects didn't prefer the opponents they were more likely to win against. They preferred the ones who genuinely smiled, even when it meant the subjects were less likely to win.[6]

Emotional correctness isn't a gimmick and, like a smile, you can't fake it. But if you authentically, genuinely want to connect with your audience, then show it—with warm and friendly nonverbal gestures, the most important of which is a great smile.

Find an emotional point of connection. A couples counselor my partner and I saw once said, "Validating isn't the same as agreeing." Great point. Saying to your loved one, "I can imagine that what I said made you really angry," isn't the same thing as saying, "You're right to be angry at me." Far from it. And, incidentally, knowing the difference appears to be one of the most important keys to a healthy and long-lasting partnership.

The same can be said for all relationships. When I'm on air talking about immigration reform or gun-safety regulations or reproductive rights, there are people in my audience who come to those conversations with their hackles already raised—conservatives who start off quite hostile to my progressive stance on such issues. So I could plow ahead with my talking points about why I think my position is right. But they probably won't hear me. To strain another metaphor from intimate-relationship-land, it's like they're on Mars and I'm on Venus. Of course they're going to dismiss my opinion if they don't even think I'm from their planet! So what's an alien perspective to do?

Emotional correctness is the way we bridge the metaphorical gaps between our life experiences, no matter how otherworldly they may seem. I may not believe in unfettered access to assault weapons, but I sure understand the desire to protect myself and my family, just like I understand not wanting to let government tread too far into our private lives.

So if I'm talking to a room full of pro-gun folks—or a planet of them for that matter—I'm not going to start by talking about how the Newtown school shooter was able to fire off one bullet every two seconds to kill twenty-six people, including twenty young children. I might start by talking about how I understand how scary the world around us is today, how every morning I put my daughter on the school bus I hug her extra hard while at the same time trying to stop myself from worrying too much—echoing and connecting with the same kinds of feelings that many of those folks probably have about their kids and loved ones. And then I might talk about how I know I can't encase my daughter in Bubble Wrap, but if there are common-sense policies that would help make her and everyone's children more safe, I'm all for 'em. And *then* I would talk about gun-control legislation. If you don't connect first, you have no hope of convincing.

11

Be the friendly person at the cocktail party. If the general lack of emotional correctness in our public discourse is driven by a hyper-competitive, antisocial, and often downright nasty culture that has infected everything from politics to business to social media, the antidote may come from remembering what it's like to be with people—and reinjecting those basic social connection skills into our other interactions.

Here I think the best metaphor is a cocktail party. If, for some reason, you've never been to a cocktail party, hurry and get to one quickly. They're awesome. You get drinks and food, often in adorably small and almost guilt-free sizes. But that's not all. According to Etiquette International, "The goal of entertaining is not the specific reason for the party, be it a new product launch or a birthday. The goal is to make others feel good—about you, a guest of honor, a product, a company, but mostly about themselves and the time they give you."[7] Imagine your speech or meeting is a party; you want people to feel good that they showed up and to have a good time.

But especially if you're not hosting the party—if you're speaking at someone else's meeting or television show or event—then the burden really is on you to be a good guest. Here's Etiquette International again:

> Guests, too, must "sing for their supper." They should always convey through their manners and actions that they are honored by all that the host has done for them, and that the host's efforts have all met with success. Guests should mingle and meet other guests. Not only is it acceptable to circulate and introduce oneself, an overburdened host will be grateful that a guest has taken the initiative to be pleasant to and interested in the others. Social interaction should not be a mine field fraught with hidden dangers that may erupt into real explosions. Remember, any offense

to another guest is a double offense because it also offends the host.[8]

This is an especially good one to remember if your host is not on the same "planet" as you—maybe they're ideologically opposed or somehow skeptical of your agenda. Well, the guests came because the host invited them—not because of you. I think about this a lot when I'm on a show like *The O'Reilly Factor* or *Hannity*. People turn on their televisions to see Bill or Sean, not me. So if I'm really rude or obnoxious to Bill or Sean, who's the audience going to side with? Not me. And if I'm rude to the other guests? Well then, I just come off as rude. If we're on the same side, then we can often see rude behavior through a tribal lens and cheer it on. That doesn't make rudeness any more acceptable, but it's thoroughly counterproductive when you're trying to win over an alien crowd.

Now, let me be clear—I'm not saying you should be a total wet noodle, looking the other way when someone says something troubling or controversial, whether on a television show or at an actual cocktail party. You can still argue back. In fact, in some cases, on some issues, one might suggest you have a moral obligation to argue back. But you can do so in a way that makes your point without making enemies, so that when "the party" is all over, folks look back and think, "I didn't agree with so-and-so, but, you know, she made some good points and was fun to talk with." That's the key to having conversations that get you further and further into the room—and into people's consciences—rather than kicked out.

Be open to being wrong. Authentic connection is a two-way street. You have to be open to having the sort of emotionally correct response to such connection that you want others to have with you. That means listening with an open heart and an open mind to people who disagree with you, which is hard, I know—but bear in mind that's exactly what you're asking people to do for you.

I'm not saying this just to be transactional, as in: if you look like you're open-minded, then they'll be more likely to be actually open-minded. No. You can't fake emotional correctness. And being open to your own fallibility, whether in terms of logic or essential human nature, is part of the realness that allows us to truly connect with others. Plus, being open to the shortcomings in your own ideas and beliefs means you can't just fake your way through trying to persuade others—you have to first persuade yourself over and over again.

I believe that strong convictions are a good thing. I personally have lots of them. But rigid dogma is disconcerting. It means our convictions are shaped more by ideology and identity than genuine feelings and reasoning. So, frankly, being open to the fact that you might be wrong doesn't just make you more emotionally correct, it makes you a more informed and thoughtful leader.

I've always felt this notion was best characterized by the brilliant statement often attributed to Mahatma Gandhi: "There goes my people. I must follow them, for I am their leader." The greatest leaders have a willingness to follow, just as the most persuasive leaders have a willingness to be persuaded.

It was also Gandhi who said, "I suppose leadership at one time meant muscles; but today it means getting along with people." Emotional correctness to the core.

Conclusion

Emotional correctness isn't for everyone—or for every moment. There are undoubtedly times when the sword of incivility is called for, when an affront or injustice is so stark and severe that the only conceivable human reaction is to lash out in response. After all, emotional correctness calls on us to recognize our fundamental, shared humanity, and by nature that means recognizing that none of us is perfect nor free from moments of often-justified rage. Emotional correctness isn't an appeal for piety. Quite the opposite. We can only authentically connect with each other if we acknowledge and are willing to share the full range of our human experiences, and not just the pretty ones.

Which is a grand way of saying I'm not perfect, and neither are any of us. As a social-movement activist, I see emotional correctness as a direct outgrowth of the nonviolent civil disobedience that defined political change from India to South Africa to the United States. But as the greatest adherents of civil disobedience have said, choosing to be nonviolent in the face of violence, choosing to be civil in the face of incivility, choosing to be compassionate in the face of injustice—these are by no means default options or even easy choices. That is precisely what makes them so revolutionary.

Dr. Martin Luther King Jr. said, "As my sufferings mounted I soon realized that there were two ways in which I could respond to my situation—either to react with bitterness or seek to transform the suffering into a creative force. I decided to follow the latter course." We all have that choice within us. No matter how much hatred and nastiness is directed our way, we have a choice as to how we respond. And our society and media contain both choices too. Sure, Twitter might make it easier to fire off anonymous hate screeds at people—but it also makes it easier to share cute cat pictures and sincere appreciations of others. Yet the choice we make is more than individual. Especially in our hypernetworked world, how we choose to be in the world, when we respond to darkness and cruelty with kindness and light, actively reshapes the world toward emotional correctness. That whole "be the change you want to see" notion isn't just about action. It's about tone, the kindness with which we treat one another. By being more emotionally correct, we create a more emotionally correct world around us.

When Nelson Mandela was elected the first black president of South Africa in 1994, one of the first things he did was fly to a remote part of the country where pro-apartheid Afrikaners were amassing arms and planning to declare an independent, all-white state. Mandela literally went right into the hotbed of all the hostility directed against him and sat down for tea with Betsie Verwoerd, the ninety-four-year-old widow of the *architect* of apartheid, the man at the center of all the hostility against Mandela and responsible for Mandela's twenty-seven-year imprisonment. If that ain't emotional correctness on the part of Mandela—and presumably Betsie Verwoerd too—then I don't know what is. This simple but profound gesture inspired the Afrikaners to disarm and slowly but surely join the path to national unity in South Africa.

Nelson Mandela certainly had a choice, like the rest of us. He could continue to let hatred fester in his heart and hostility mount in his rhetoric. But then again, if he really wanted to heal a nation and move forward with unity of purpose and country, as opposed to ugliness and division, did he have any other choice? And if our goal is really to solve our problems as a country and function as a healthy democracy, do we actually have any choice but to try and find compassion for each other and, ultimately, common ground?

There aren't a lot of New Yorkers who watch Fox News, but whenever I'm in more conservative parts of America, I get stopped by countless people who recognize me from television. The interactions usually follow the same pattern, with folks saying to me something along the lines of, "I don't agree with everything you say, but I enjoy watching you. You seem nice." My all-time favorite variation on this theme was a woman who stopped me in the middle of a rainstorm at Disney World (while I was encased in a plastic rain poncho) and said, "You make me want to pull my hair out a lot of the time, but, ya know, sometimes you make good points. And you're fun."

Emotional correctness isn't a state of being—like I said, no one is perfect, certainly I'm not, and I suspect even Mother Teresa had an outburst here or there. Emotional correctness is a state of *becoming*, of constantly striving toward more authentic empathy with those around us, especially those with whom we disagree. That doesn't mean abandoning that in which we believe.

Ours is a world filled with massive gulfs of inequality and injustice, and the more people work to bridge those gulfs, the better the world will be. But we cannot bridge them alone. We know from history that the greatest injustices require the greatest responses, with mass social movements and ordinary people pushing for extraordinary change. We need more people engaged in change than ever before, certainly more than are engaged currently. Just sitting around preaching to the choir—and denigrating the other side— will not alter the dynamics of understanding and engagement to bring millions and millions more to the cause of social change. But one by one, if we can build bridges of compassion and find ways to really listen to each other, a society rooted in emotional correctness will emerge. And while that certainly will make us all more effective at talking to our extended families and selling our business propositions and products, emotional correctness will also make those of us who believe in peace and justice and equal opportunity for all even greater advocates for change—change that the vast majority of people support when they are actually able to hear us.

Notes

1. Karen Stephenson, "What Knowledge Tears Apart, Networks Make Whole," *Internal Communication Focus*, no. 36 (1998) http://www .netform.com/html/icf.pdf.

2. Elaine Chan and Jaideep Sengupta, "Insincere Flattery Actually Works: A Dual Attitudes Perspective," *Journal of Marketing Research*, 47 (2010): 122–133.

3. "Oprah Talks to Bill Clinton," *O, The Oprah Magazine*, August 2004, http://www.oprah.com/omagazine/Oprah-Interviews -President-Bill-Clinton/1.

4. Amy J. C. Cuddy, Matthew Kohut, and John Neffinger, "Connect, Then Lead," *Harvard Business Review*, July–August 2013, http://hbr .org/2013/07/connect-then-lead/.

5. Erin A. Heerey and Danielle M. Shore, "The Value of Genuine and Polite Smiles," *Emotion* 11, no. 1 (February 2011): 169–74.

6. Erin A. Heerey and Helen M. Crossley, "Predictive and Reactive Mechanisms in Smile Reciprocity," *Psychological Science* 24, no. 8 (August 9, 2013) 1446–1455.

7. "Hospitable Hosts, Gracious Guests," Etiquette International, accessed January 2014, http://www.etiquetteinternational.com /Articles/HostsGuests.aspx.

8. See note 7 above.

2.

WHY I NEVER TELL ANYONE MY AGE

Nisha Chittal

When I was twenty-two, I was working as a strategist at a digital agency, and I went on a business trip to Miami to give a presentation to a major Fortune 500 client on our recommendations for the company's social media strategy. For weeks, I brainstormed ideas and slaved over creating the perfect PowerPoint deck for the meeting. The presentation, which I participated in with three more senior colleagues, went well. Afterward, as one of my colleagues and I waited for a taxi back to our hotel, my coworker, who was in her early thirties, congratulated me on a job well done and asked, "By the way, how old are you?" When I responded that I was twenty-two, her tone changed. She immediately squealed, "Oh my God, but you're such a baby! And they're letting you present to clients!"

Whereas a minute ago, she had been impressed with my presentation and my composure in front of major clients, now, having found out my age, she suddenly could only see me as just another twenty-two-year-old: too young to be taking on such a level of responsibility at work. From that day on, no meeting was complete without her making reference to how I was "so young!"—regardless of how good a job I was doing.

A year later, at twenty-three, I was at a new job, leading social media efforts for a cable TV channel. A colleague introduced me to another, older coworker, and said, "Nisha is our new social media manager. She sits in the office down the hall." The older coworker responded, "Oh yes, I walked by and saw you in there, and I was like, wow, I didn't know they started letting twelve-year-olds work here!"

Welcome to the new age discrimination?

Every woman knows this to be true: when you tell someone your age, you give them the power to decide how you're perceived. No matter your qualifications, people are predisposed to judge what you are really "worth" to them based on your age. The point of someone asking your age is almost always so that the asker can make a judgment about you based on that age—what other reason is there? Finding out your age is a way for people to size you up, put you in a specific box, determine their expectations for you, and decide whether you meet them sufficiently. For women, age unfairly becomes a standard by which society determines worth: Past a certain age, a woman is viewed as less important, less worthy of attention. Younger than a certain age, a woman is also viewed as less valuable, especially in the workplace—young women are typically viewed as too naïve, too inexperienced. And many young women are often stuck longer than they'd like in intern or administrative roles because they allegedly lack the "experience" (which I've found is often just code for age and seniority) needed to move beyond entry level.

For better or worse, the practice of women hiding their age is nothing new. Look at any number of movies and TV shows, and you'll see countless jokes about women and age, and countless female characters hiding and even lying about their age. In *Sex and the City*, Charlotte York declares on her thirty-sixth birthday: "I've thought about it, and I've decided I'm sticking at thirty-five." She later adds, "Men are more interested in meeting thirty-five-year-olds." In Judd Apatow's 2012 film *This Is 40*, Leslie Mann's character pretends she's turning thirty-nine and later gets caught lying about her birth year on paperwork at her doctor's office. In September 2013, Sarah Silverman pointedly joked she was "embarrassed" to discover she was forty-two after a slew of ageist barbs were directed at her during a Comedy Central roast of James Franco: "Because it's personal, that is just so woman-based . . . I feel like your joke is that I'm still alive. My crime is not dying."

America's youth-obsessed culture tends to favor the young, and women of a certain age indisputably face unfair biases, particularly in the workforce, where some 65 percent of boomer workers report facing age discrimination,[1] and a recent case affecting workers over forty went all the way to the Supreme Court.[2] *More* magazine reported in 2008 that older women were filing more age discrimination complaints with the Equal Employment Opportunity Commission (EEOC) than ever before.[3] In 2013 in *Salon*, writer Tira Hirpaz summed up what it felt like to be an over-fifty woman in the eyes of society: "If you want to make a person invisible, just put them in the shoes of an over-fifty woman and abracadabra, watch them disappear."[4] And though I'm still in my twenties—when it's hard to garner sympathy for being young in a world that places a premium on youth—I never, ever tell anyone my age if I can avoid it.

I've been writing online for seven years. I work on social media strategy at a major cable news network and previously worked at another cable TV network; I regularly speak on panels and at conferences and have had my writing published in several online publications, magazines, and in two anthologies. I say this not to brag, but to give you a better understanding of what people are reacting to when they then find out my age. I do everything I can to make it the last thing they discover about me—there are only so many infantilizing "You're just a baby!" responses you can hear before you learn the subject is best avoided.

I am not interested in being anyone's measuring stick. In my experience, older people often use the moment to reminisce about what they were like at my age or to give me unsolicited advice from their newfound position of seniority. "You're twenty-two? When I was your age I was still partying every night!" is a statement I've heard many a time (for the record, I do not party every night). That I don't fit their expectations for someone of my age—or their memory of what they were doing at my age—can be flattering but also embarrassing, and I am never quite sure how to respond. Should I have not accomplished anything at my age? Their surprise at a young person charging ahead in her career suggests to me an underlying assumption that most twentysomethings haven't amounted to much—an idea that seems to be more and more common in this postrecession era. My age places me in the "millennial" generation, a title I have quickly come to despise for all its baggage and negative connotations. *Millennial* is a word that for many people a generation or so ahead of mine seems to conjure up images of young people who are lazy, entitled, attached to their devices, incompetent, and unable to do a job well, or even hold down a serious office job. These days, youth isn't so much desirable as it is loaded with connotations of inexperience, laziness, and naïveté.

Want proof? Look no further than your nearest newsstand. Earlier this year, *Time* magazine featured a cover story on millennials, the headline of which proclaimed: "The me me me generation: millennials are lazy, entitled narcissists who still live with their

people who find that a handful of lazy workers have given an entire generation an unfairly poor reputation. And so the more people tried to find out my age, the more I knew that they were, consciously or unconsciously, looking for a number so they could make a judgment—and I refused to give that power to them. Still do.

After a while, I found that hiding my age was really working well for me. People were forced to judge me on my work alone, and doing good work led many people to start assuming I was older than I was. And I knew better than to correct them. I didn't—and still don't—want everyone I meet to view me through that filter, layering their impressions of millennials on me before they know anything about my work.

Refusing to discuss age in the workplace would certainly be a time-saver for all concerned. The young women I know are smart, capable, and extremely hardworking—and many of them are leading a new wave of innovation in the digital world. They're digital directors and digital experts at nonprofits, magazines, TV networks, and more. Some are entrepreneurs who have started their own successful companies before they've even turned twenty-five. They work long hours, generate big results, and are dedicated to building successful careers. They're not looking for praise or a pat on the back; they're just looking for the respect of their colleagues and peers. And they're all tired of the judgment and even ridicule they get from older coworkers who find out they're only twenty-two, twenty-five, or twenty-seven. "You're *how old*?" is a line most of us hear often, and we dread hearing it just as much as many women over forty would.

The irony is, while older workers love to judge a young worker's age, lots of millennials are getting hired in high-level roles because of their digital experience. Gripe all you want about millennials' supposed faults, but many young people with a few years of experience under their belts are becoming highly desirable hires for companies and organizations looking to innovate, try new things, and adapt to the ever-changing digital landscape. Frequently, those millennials are managing teams that include employees who are older than they are. This is usually not a problem until coworkers find out their manager may be younger than them, which can make working relationships awkward and cause a few bruised egos. Ambitious young professionals have all the more incentive to hide their age.

As I started talking to friends about my frustrations, similar stories came pouring out of the woodwork. It turns out many young, successful women follow the same rule: they avoid telling anyone at work their age at all costs. They have college degrees, possibly advanced degrees, big ambitions, and a desire to work hard, hustle, and prove themselves. They also take great pains to never reveal their age to a coworker.

One of my good friends—I'll call her Sally—is twenty-six and holds a high-level role at a think tank in Washington, DC. She spoke about hiding her age at her second job out of college:

> Not only was I coming in as a member of the senior staff, I was the second-youngest person on staff . . . Once they learned how old I was, I felt like they lost some respect for me. It wasn't that I was doing my job any differently, it's just that, because of my age, I suddenly lacked the authority I once had. People make split judgments about you based on age, which is silly. I've seen twentysomethings do amazing things and reinvent the world, and I've seen people with thirty years of work experience under their belt do the exact same thing.

My friend Meredith Fineman, who started her own company at the age of twenty-four, recently wrote in *Harvard Business Review* about her frustration at constantly being asked how old she is, and how, despite her professional accomplishments, people want to judge her more on her age than anything else. "When I am asked that question, it's usually to gauge if, at recently 26, the fact that I've had my own company, FinePoint Digital PR, for nearly two years is admirable, suspect, or something else," Fineman wrote.[7] She said that to avoid dealing with people's reactions when they found out she was twenty-six, she simply declined to answer, often responding with the old-fashioned "A lady never tells her age."

Another friend, who is twenty-seven and the digital director at a prominent nonprofit in New York City, says, "I'm still hesitant to discuss my age because I manage people who are older than me. I started off never disclosing my age or biographical details that would help pinpoint how old I was. This wasn't triggered by anything specific other than a fear of not being taken seriously. As I've climbed up the corporate ladder, I've relaxed a lot of my rules on this, but I've had a few people point out my age. But guess what? If you want a 'digital expert' these days, chances are that they're a young person!"

She, like others, feels that determination and hard work should matter more than her age. Jen Nedeau, a twenty-nine-year-old digital media expert in Washington, DC, told me: "I've felt judged for my age at various points in my career. I hate that I have to prove myself over and over again to a variety of people in a variety of settings . . . You are always going to have to show people your worth, and once they begin to value you, the relationship can change dramatically for the better."

Unlike most other young, high-achieving women, though, Nedeau says, "I'm a pretty open book about my age. I'm proud of where I've gotten in a short time. Certain environments are more difficult than others to engage with as a young woman, but having a sense of pride in yourself can help you move past anyone who tries to invalidate you because of your age or gender . . . No matter what, I've made a promise to myself that I'm not going to apologize for my success or take a seat on the sidelines in order to accommodate other people."

The other young women I spoke to agreed that they were proud of the things they'd achieved in a short period of time, but most were still reluctant to share their age at work. Young women who felt comfortable publicly sharing their age in professional settings were few and far between, and they often felt more comfortable doing so when they were in a company that was younger. "I currently work in a very young office, where I'm one of the older people in the firm, but in the past, I was one of the youngest in the room," Nedeau said.

Each young woman I talked to kept returning to the same point: that no matter how hard she worked, how polished her presentations, how good her results, how many people she managed, when coworkers found out her age, that became the first thing people associated with her, ahead of her credentials, work, and résumé. Her success was worth less because she was so young. Older coworkers who made jabs about younger colleagues seemed to feel that they may not be able to avoid having this millennial in the office, but they could make themselves feel a little better and undermine her credibility by reminding her how young she is. And that's exactly why more and more young women are subscribing to the idea that has for so long been the dreaded lot of older women: to get ahead you have to keep your age a secret, no matter how much you excel in your work.

And so I say to my fellow twentysomething women who have ambitious goals and big plans to get there, here's my secret to getting ahead early in your career: never tell anyone your age. You'll feel more empowered and more in control of your professional image when you don't let people reduce you to a number—the second they know your age, they start to judge you. Instead, show people your work, your experience, and your ideas. I'm certainly not suggesting you lie about your age. But I am saying that you'll have a leg up at work if you let your experience and smarts dictate how people perceive you—factors that are so much more important than your age.

As you prepare to enter the working world, or if you have already entered it but struggle to prove yourself to coworkers who take you less seriously because of your young age, take a look at the steps I took to prove myself. Nearly everything I did was related to leveraging the power of the Internet and social media. The beautiful thing about social media is that it has flattened our world, brought our networks online, and made everyone more accessible. While there are downsides to the always-on, always-accessible culture, the upside for you is that social media platforms have made it easier to connect with almost anyone you want to meet. When I was starting out, I was in college in rural central Illinois with dreams of a career in DC and New York, but I knew no one in those cities and had no established networks to fall back on. Instead, I turned to the Internet to make my own way. Here are a few of the things that worked for me—and may work for you as well as you establish yourself in your field.

I started by reading every blog I could. I read career blogs, political blogs, media blogs, tech blogs, everything. Whatever interests you, read the blogs and websites in your field. Especially career blogs: read them all. Devour them. When you're a student, the thought of extra reading when you already have hundreds of pages of political theory to read can be daunting, but the payoff is worth it. Read everything you find with a hunger to learn everything you can about the working world before you've entered it. College, especially a liberal arts degree, will not teach you all the career skills you need to be effective in the workplace. My liberal arts education was fascinating and enriching, and made me a better writer and critical thinker. But it did not teach me how to transition into the corporate world, what the rules of the working world are, how to effectively network, and how to successfully job hunt. We could make the argument that our higher education system is broken because it doesn't equip young people with the skills they need to transition from college to the workforce. Be that as it may, don't let "I didn't know" be your excuse. There are a million career and hiring experts writing online, giving away free advice. Read as many of them as you can. You can learn all of that from the Internet!

After years of reading blogs, I decided to take a risk and start a blog of my own. Writing a polished, professional blog that showcases your ideas, your interests, and your smarts—and growing an audience with it—is one of the single best things you can do to prove yourself at a young age. On a blog, people learn about—and learn from—your area of expertise, and readers see your ideas before they know your age. Even if you're not quite a subject matter expert yet, a blog is a powerful tool for discussion, writing, and ideas. What's more, visitors to a blog form their first impression based on the quality of what they read. If they do find out your age later down the road, you've already proved what you have to offer, and your age becomes less important. So whatever you're passionate about—food, technology, books, politics, photography, whatever—start a blog and showcase what you know. Don't mention anywhere on said blog that you're a college senior, recent college grad, or anything that marks you as young—just write about your interests, and let people form an impression of you based on your writing.

I've seen many a college student's WordPress blog die because they felt no one was reading, and updating it felt like a chore that would never pay off. The key to a successful blog is understanding that a blog can't grow in a vacuum. You need to go out and find an audience after you hit "Publish." Every time you write a post, share it on Facebook and Twitter. Those other bloggers you've been reading? Comment on their blog posts: leave thoughtful comments that add to the discussion, and make sure to include a link to your blog in your signature. If you're writing about a niche topic, find groups on Facebook and LinkedIn or chats and hashtags on Twitter that relate to it and engage in discussions and share your new posts as well. While keeping a blog does take a bit of time, it can have a huge payoff in terms of the connections you build.

Even if the time commitment of a blog isn't for you, Twitter is a must for everyone. First of all, let's dispense with the obvious and very tired "what I ate for breakfast" jokes. Anyone who thinks Twitter is just a social network for narcissistic oversharers is, quite frankly, doing themselves a great disservice. I see Twitter as the most valuable networking tool I have. Most people greatly underestimate the professional value Twitter offers. It has truly made the world flatter by allowing people to have two-way interaction with just about anyone. You may not be able to find an e-mail address for that person you want to connect with, but you can find them on Twitter. Start a professional Twitter account under your real name, follow people who interest you and people in your industry, and tweet links to articles that you value. Reply to people you want to get to know and engage them in conversations. Once you've established a connection on Twitter, turn those connections into real relationships off-line: e-mail, ask questions, go for coffee. Build relationships with a diverse array of people and don't concern yourself with whether these people can "help" you with something in your career right at this moment.

Don't ever, ever be afraid to cold e-mail someone you want to get to know. Whatever internal fears you have about cold e-mailing someone, get over it. Seriously, lean in! You have absolutely nothing to lose and possibly everything to gain. My sophomore year in college, I was looking for summer internships in journalism, but I lived in Illinois and didn't have the money to do an unpaid internship in New York, where most big media companies were headquartered. Instead, I looked at all the political blogs I read and identified one of my favorites, a political website for women called Citizen Jane Politics. They hadn't advertised any open internships, but I found the editor's e-mail address on the site and wrote her, telling her about myself and how much I loved the site. I asked whether she needed a summer intern who could work remotely. That single e-mail landed me not just a summer internship but also led eventually to a yearlong position as associate editor of the website.

Since then I've cold e-mailed countless editors with freelance pitches, as well as numerous other people I just wanted to connect with or learn from. It gets less and less scary each time. Sure, not everyone responds, and you should brace yourself for the fact that some of your e-mails will go unreturned. Editors may be drowning in e-mails and lose track of yours. Or, maybe they're just not interested. A nonresponse is the worst that can happen, and if it does, move on to the next one and don't take it personally.

Network everywhere, and say yes to opportunities. Most people groan when they hear they have to "network." But where they hear "networking" and imagine forced, awkward small talk and begging for a job at giant networking events, I see a way to constantly be meeting new people—and making new friends. Networking shouldn't be any more or less than simply that: meeting people and making friends. A former *Cosmopolitan* editor and author recently said in an interview, "Networking isn't everything—*it's the only* *thing.*"[8] Don't wait until you're looking for a job to network—you should be networking all the time. Say yes to every invitation. Go to coffee or lunch with someone in your industry who you'd like to get to know better. Go to those group happy hours even if you are nervous about showing up and not knowing anyone. Go, and you'll come out of it with new connections and new friends. There will likely be a time later in life when you start to receive so many invitations that you have to be selective in choosing which events to attend. But when you're starting out and need to meet people, that's not the time to be selective. Say yes to the opportunities that come your way even if they seem scary, daunting, or nerve-racking—even if you'd rather be home watching Netflix than be at a conference forcing yourself to talk to people you don't know.

Remember that networking is not about trying to seek out and meet only those people who can do something for you. Reframe your view of networking: think about it as just meeting people and building new relationships, whether people seem like they could help you or not. Think about how you can help the people you meet, too. If you approach networking with the narrow mind-set of only finding those people who can help you and ignoring all others, you will surely be a networking failure.

Get comfortable with a little bit of self-promotion. Nearly every woman I know—me included—feels a little uneasy about promoting her own work. *New York*'s Kat Stoeffel recently wrote in a piece on women's struggles with self-promotion, "My female colleagues tweet, 'Here's this little thing I made,' with a link to an article months in the making."[9] I can't tell you how many times I've heard a woman share news of a hard-earned promotion, or a new job, launch, or project, but preface it with, "Not to toot my own horn, but . . ." And I often hear young women hesitantly share an idea with, "Well, I'm only just out of college, but . . ." This kind of self-deprecating language has got to go—it diminishes our own hard work and efforts. When you've put hours, weeks, even months into a project, there's nothing wrong with feeling proud of your creation and owning your success. And you will never hear a man use qualifiers like this when talking about his ideas or his accomplishments—men simply go for it and share their ideas as if they're the best damn ideas anyone's ever had! (Even when they're not.) For women, and especially younger women, it's important that we don't downplay our own ideas and achievements. While it may feel gauche to brag about your work, it's important to remind yourself that a man would never hesitate to do the same thing, and that often leads to men getting more visibility and more opportunities. If you want a seat at the table, it won't be handed to you. You have to show your value, show why you deserve it, and ask for it.

Finally, always fake it till you make it. It may be a cliché, but the most valuable piece of advice I can give is that people will give you the amount of respect you show yourself. Even if you're a just-out-of-college twentysomething and you feel like you have no idea what you're doing, no one has to know that. Act as if you feel confident at work, and soon you'll feel confident. How you carry yourself and present yourself to the world is one of the greatest ways you can shape how people perceive you. For twentysomethings, it's crucial to avoid presenting yourself as a Hannah Horvath–esque twentysomething mess (even if you feel that way inside, which is okay!). Instead, carry yourself well, own your accomplishments, and fake a healthy confidence in yourself, your ideas, and your work. Act as though you deserve to be respected, and your colleagues and peers will respect you. Not everyone is naturally confident—I've yet to meet someone who is—but faking it and presenting yourself to the world as smart and deserving of respect no matter your age is the fastest way to getting there.

Notes

1. Kerry Hannon, "How Women Job Seekers Can Beat Age Discrimination," *NextAvenue.org*, September 27, 2012, http://www.nextavenue.org/blog/how-women-job-seekers-can-beat-age-discrimination.

2. Lisa McElroy, "Supreme Court Takes a 'DIG' at Age Discrimination," *AARP Blog*, October 16, 2013, http://blog.aarp.org/2013/10/16/supreme-court-takes-a-dig-at-age-discrimination.

3. Amy Engeler, "Older and Out: Age Discrimination in the Workplace," *MORE*, April 6, 2009, http://www.more.com/news/womens-issues/older-and-out-age-discrimination-workplace.

4. Tira Hirpaz, "Women Over 50 Are Invisible," *Salon*, April 5, 2013, http://www.salon.com/2013/04/05/wanna_know_what_its_like_to_disappear_try_being_a_woman_over_50_partner/.

5. Joel Stein, "Millennials, The Me Me Me Generation," *TIME*, May 20, 2013, http://content.time.com/time/magazine/article/0,9171,2143001,00.html.

6. Robin Marantz Henig, "What Is It About 20-Somethings?" *New York Times*, August 18, 2010, http://www.nytimes.com/2010/08/22/magazine/22Adulthood-t.html.

7. Meredith Fineman, "Just How Old Are You?" *Harvard Business Review*, March 29, 2013, http://blogs.hbr.org/2013/03/just-how-old-are-you/.

8. Kate White, "The Secrets of My Success," *DailyWorth*, October 21, 2013, http://www.dailyworth.com/posts/2200-7-career-tips-from-a-magazine-mogul/2.

9. Kat Stoeffel, "Here's This Thing I Wrote About Women and Self-Promotion," *New York*, September 25, 2013, http://nymag.com/thecut/2013/09/heres-this-thing-i-wrote-about-self-promotion.html.

3.
STARTING FROM THE BOTTOM

Jenna Wortham

I didn't start out wanting to be a journalist, let alone one who worked at one of the biggest publications in the world. As the first person in my family to go to a reputable, sleepaway, four-year university, my career goals were simple. I wanted a job with a salary and good benefits, especially dental, because I have a terrible sweet tooth. But it didn't work out that way, at least not at first. Everything about college baffled me; nothing I studied or did adequately prepared me for figuring out how to carve out a successful life for myself after graduation.

Most of my friends had five-year plans; some even claimed to have ten-year plans. Many had at least chosen a professional category to pursue: law, medicine, business. Me, I made the plan to have no plan. I was loose, almost pathologically determined not to commit to something too soon. Sometimes that was terrifying. I'd be listening to my premed friends talking about their top picks for residency, and a wave of panic would subsume me, and I would spend the rest of the day dazed, not sure if I should be doing what they were doing, if I was making a series of terrible tactical life errors that would haunt me for the rest of my days. But I'd seen enough *Felicity* to know that it would take some time to figure out my life plan, and I felt confident that one would materialize eventually. I had gotten myself into college, and if I left with a degree in hand, that felt good enough for me, so I focused on what I considered to be the colloquial college experience instead. I signed up for a sculpture class that mostly involved sneaking into a local scrap yard late at night and picking through junk and old electronics for things we might fashion into other things. I lived with a whole mess of girls in a tiny apartment right above four cute engineers who liked to take our door off and use it to play beer pong. I signed up for swim class and then dropped out. I signed up for crew and then dropped out. The unending options were unnerving, but I had a blind confidence that my haphazard process of eliminating subjects, concepts, and areas of study would somehow, eventually, deposit me at the foot of my future career and path. I took a class on riot grrrl zines taught by a grad student who would knit hats during class and hand out mixtapes of Bratmobile songs. I bounced from the biology department to the anthropology department and later applied for a semester abroad in London studying public health. When I came back, I moved off campus with my boyfriend and enrolled in graduate classes in grassroots media.

But as graduation slowly started to solidify from a murky concept into a rapidly approaching date, I began to realize that the degree that I was going to wind up with—a combination of biology, lit classes, and anthropology—didn't seem to be a natural fit for anything—interesting or otherwise—on the job market. At night, anxiety made camp in my body, keeping me awake as I fretted over what I could do to make money and where I would live.

Some of my classmates and friends were filling out applications for the Peace Corps and Teach For America; others were preparing for graduate school. Most had gotten help securing an office job in their hometowns and were preparing to move home. None of it appealed to me. College had taught me how to properly prepare ramen and hot chocolate in a hot pot balanced on a plastic crate, how to use new tools like Napster and Kazaa, the delicate balance of winning an argument in lecture that both charmed the professor and didn't annoy my peers, the joy of diner food at two a.m., and the art of crafting the perfect away message to leave on IM while away from my computer. Social cultivation, self-presentation, cultural interests, yes. Professional direction or any sense of how to use what I'd learned over the last four years, no. Facebook was just starting to catch on around college campuses and the FOMO was intense and real as people started posting updates about new jobs or European summer trips. I couldn't pin my future down in that exact moment, so I made the decision to delay it. I'd always been able to figure out a plan, and I knew that money was the key to future independence. The thing is, I'd had all kinds of jobs before, but none were jobs that I wanted to return to after graduation. But I figured working was better than not working, so I set about getting a kind of job that wouldn't necessarily be one that I'd have forever—just for the near term. That decision not to rush into a decision, the uncertainty of continuing to cherry-pick between classes and sampling different ideas and potential career paths, seemed terrifying, but in hindsight, it helped establish in my early twenties the pattern of leaps and risks that I would have to make later on as my career began to take shape. I'd always worked, I'd always hustled. And that instinct to get work and build up some momentum, even if I didn't yet have a clear sense toward what, would wind up serving me as well as, if not better than, the sum of all the classes I'd sat through and papers I'd handed in.

The thing I remember most about my first job were the roses. They arrived a few days before Valentine's Day in big, soggy cardboard boxes. We sat on upside-down white buckets in a freezing walk-in refrigerator, stripping off thorns and leaves and wrapping the roses up in bundles that we would hand to harried spouses and lovers when they rushed through the door later that week. I was sixteen and only worked on weekends, so I didn't earn very much, but I spent what little money I made on teen things like crop tops, lip gloss, CDs, and movie tickets. It was some help to my mother, who worked full-time to support my older sister and me, but mostly it was liberating. After that, I always had a job. In high school, I picked up shifts after school as a hostess at a sports bar called Damon's. One exhausting summer, I worked at a camp during the day and stocked books overnight at Barnes & Noble. But cashing those paychecks every month was the first step toward self-sufficiency, which in my case was a necessity but also imbued me with the importance of independence, financially or otherwise. So I decided to look for work that would generate cash, and fast, while I got the rest of my life into some semblance of order. Even though I still wasn't sure what I wanted to do with my future, I had a glimmer of an idea that it would be difficult to quantify, something not currently defined or known to most of the people I knew growing up—other army brats and kids whose parents worked in Washington, DC. I knew that resiliency and elbow grease would go a long way.

During my last year of school at the University of Virginia, I was spending most of my time downtown, away from campus, and I had gotten to know a few servers from the restaurant scene. I'd heard from a few of them that business was good. They sometimes made as much as $300 on a good night, which was my share of the rent at the time, and it seemed too good to pass up. I was hired at the first place I applied, a super-fancy French restaurant known for its handmade pastas and locavore approach even before that was a popular trend, mostly because everyone else had quit the day I walked in. In hindsight, that should have been a red flag, but I was excited by the prospect of a new challenge, and of course, the money. I remember standing there, sparse résumé in hand, when Roman, the bartender-slash-manager, asked me if I was up for helping him run the restaurant that night. They were expecting a full house of people and we'd make bank, he promised, since he and I would be the only two waiters splitting tips. I agreed, and he tossed me a black server apron and told me to start setting tables. Before that night, I hadn't done more than have a few friends over for dinner, and I was wholly unprepared to gracefully and elegantly take care of an entire dining room asking for recommendations on dishes like sweetbreads and ordering cappuccinos that I had to make myself, on a rickety machine in the back. The chaos was so unnerving, so extreme, that I blacked out most of the night. I can remember a few things, in no particular order: I sweated through my entire outfit, spilled hot tea on a guy that I recognized from around school, and corked a very expensive bottle of wine that I tried to open tableside. There's no real way to quantify the hellish stress of standing next to a table that is quietly debating whether to share an entrée or get two different ones to try while the people across the room are glaring at you to come take their drink order. The ever-evolving mathematics of orchestrating the arrival of food, drinks, checks, and new customers was exhilarating and exhausting. It was like a never-ending game of Diner Dash, relentless and insufferable. But I didn't get any orders wrong, and I managed to maintain my cool over the course of the night. After the last customer left, we locked up and opened a bottle of champagne and toasted ourselves for not going down in flames. That night, I'm pretty sure I pocketed enough money to cover my rent, and a nice amount of cash to cover expenses for a few weeks. It was liberating in a way that my college classes had not been until that point, and the crisp bills felt like a step toward something else after college, savings to travel, a safety net to cover my bills while I ran errands, or, who knows, got hired to do part-time work, for a photographer or a filmmaker, perhaps. And I was done in time to go meet my friends for last call. I was hooked.

Until that moment, nothing in college made much sense. I found the entire four-year process to be such a mysterious ritual that waitressing, by comparison, was a relief. I struggled to fit into the collegiate dance of a southern school that counted wearing ties and sundresses to football games among one of its traditions. It was a special breed of performative adulthood I wasn't quite ready for— am still probably not ready for. But waitressing was different. It was something I could figure out, a game that I had the instructions for. And it was hard, but also simple. If you worked hard enough and paid attention, you could do anything, make anything work. You could handle any table, any crisis, so long as you kept your wits about you, and there was something incredibly reassuring about that. The hustle also appealed to me, as did the mental calculus that you have to do for each table to plot out the course of their meal. Of course, then there was the money, which felt like a freedom from the servitude of being a struggling college student.

Most people I worked with weren't planning on being servers forever. Some were in school like me; others were using the money to supplement their day jobs as artists or dancers. I had a fantasy of a future self that worked as a photographer, a social activist, a documentary filmmaker, a vaccine researcher, or even as a chemist. But the clearer it became that I had no idea what to do after college, the more appealing waitressing as a stopgap became. A reliable job and skill set that would be applicable in any city I landed in sounded like a smart way to start my postgraduation life. I knew it paid well, and I would have my days free to intern, freelance, or do odd jobs.

And so I shook Roman's hand and accepted that job and others like it while I figured out how to be an adult human and turn the various side projects and freelance gigs I was doing into something resembling a career. The job quickly became a priority, pulling me away from college dances and parties, but I didn't mind. I started telling people that I was waitressing to save up enough money to go to California, which eventually became true. People's reactions to my announcement became a Rorschach test that was fairly accurate at predicting the length of time we'd be in touch after graduation. It sounded cool enough to a few of my closest friends, who decided to do the same, and we all began to prepare ourselves for a great migration out West. We dreamed of open skies, a chilled-out vibe, and the space to become fully realized, whatever we thought that meant. It wasn't much of a plan but it felt like a better plan than most people had, which involved getting a regular office job. But by this time, my grassroots publishing class had begun to work its way under my skin, and I liked the way it took root there. I pictured myself running a similar enterprise someday. We published a magazine each semester, and planning out the issues, the front-of-the-book stories, features, and profiles that we would include was exciting in a way I didn't even know was possible. In those classes, the beginnings of an idea took shape, if only I could figure out how to finance it. The reality that I had spent the last four years doing everything but studying literature, writing, and reading started to weigh on me, even though all of those areas interested me the most. But I figured I would stockpile cash, leather jackets, and skinny jeans, move to a city, live in a one-room apartment, and work and intern for free in exchange for experience points. Simple enough, right?

Waitressing, first in Virginia, and then in San Francisco, was much more than a buffer, much more than a cushion of cash that paid the bills and allowed me to afford small animal comforts like nice bottles of wine and occasional overnight trips down the coast. Learning to collaborate with strangers, along with the ability to interface with other people—read them, anticipate their reactions, learn how to adapt and react to almost any situation—better prepared me for the kind of future that I always pictured that I wanted. It was something I'd never expected to learn from a restaurant. I worried that my lack of a serious-sounding job title or fellowship would harm my chances at success in the future, but it turned out that waitressing was my last first job, the one that would carry me through until I landed at the *New York Times*. I didn't realize it at the time, but I learned almost everything I needed to know to be a successful human while working in restaurants, possibly even more than I learned in college. The bone-breaking hard work of hoisting trays of food and glasses and the relentless charm and poise that is required for the service industry primed me for years of long hours interning for little to no money and a willingness and openness to experiences that would help me inch closer to the dream goal of someday running or writing for a magazine. It's the one job of the half dozen I've had that I miss on occasion.

People ask me all the time for career advice. They're interested in figuring out how to carve out their own path, whether forging a future in a world that is rapidly shifting—often beneath their feet—is possible, and how much weight a traditional education carries in a world that is increasingly defined by skills and expertise that is still being shaped. Most people are worried that they aren't doing enough or that their social or online footprint isn't big enough or distinguished enough. When you're first starting out, you probably won't get the job you want. You probably don't even know what the job you will be happiest with looks like because, chances are, it isn't around yet. Or its definition will be so fluid and flux it doesn't warrant proper categorization or title. And it'll probably take a while to get it. Ten years ago, I thought I'd be a magazine writer or a columnist. Today, I'm a business reporter and sometimes a columnist, a videographer, a producer. I do all kinds of things I never thought I would get to do, and it changes constantly because the field I work in is evolving underneath my feet. Being lean, being flexible, being agile enough to evolve has helped keep me afloat. Paying attention to my environment and making sure I'm a part of it, rather than a tourist in it, has also helped. Everyone has their own path, and not all paths look alike. This gets harder and harder to remember when we are all preening and performing on social media, celebrating the highlights—new jobs, promotions, the lists we were recognized on, and the articles about our successes—and ignoring the lowlights. The struggle is real, and it touches everyone at some point, but we're inclined to ignore it on the way up. It's easier that way. But comparing myself to other people has never gotten me anywhere—I never wanted to be like other people, and that's still true, even now. I didn't start out with much by way of external resources—I didn't come from family money, or resources, or anything else that might help me get a jump in the media world. But I was fairly confident that I could figure out anything on the fly (and never let on otherwise) and that I could do it beautifully. Those were the stories I told myself to live, to keep my head above water when it felt like I should give up or maybe try something else. I trusted my gut, I trusted my instinct, and I trusted that I could make it work, which were the main keepsakes I picked up from waitressing.

It's been more than five years since my last shift, but the things I learned have stayed with me over the years. Here are some of those lessons and reflections:

Have a plan B. Have a plan A, but really, have a solid plan B in your back pocket at all times. Plan Bs don't have to be permanent. They don't have to be anything but what they are: a backup. A backup isn't a sign of failure; it's an escape hatch, an ejector seat, or a parachute that floats you to the next thing. A way to ensure that you can still pay your bills because life is very likely to take you unexpected places, and you have to be able to know that you have some kind of net that you can fall back on. For me, it was much easier moving to San Francisco at the tender age of twenty-one to look for work and explore internships knowing that, no matter what, I could always waitress. The same was true when I moved to New York a few years later. Even though I had a job, I reasoned that if it didn't work out, I could pick up some shifts somewhere while I figured out my next moves. That confidence grew out of a sense of self-sufficiency and helped me make moves that I otherwise might have been too intimidated to make. When I interviewed for my job at the *Times*, I was down to the last hundred dollars in my checking account. I took unpaid time off from work to travel to New York and was fairly certain that I wouldn't have a job when I got back. The thought of going broke and losing my job was terrifying, but I rationalized that I'd always be able to make enough money to get by and I couldn't let that be the reason to stop me from seeing the possibility of a new life through.

You already know so much. Think about it—you do! You already know so much. In fact, you probably know enough to do the job you want to do. But respect the process. And know that no matter how much you do know, you can always learn more. Be willing to learn more. See what you can absorb from someone else, even if they haven't been doing it as long as you. Just observing my coworkers from time to time has taught me a lot about their own techniques for dealing with difficult customers, smoothing over rough experiences, charming people into ordering a second bottle of wine, and, particularly, being a reporter. Every day presents a new challenge, a new assignment, a new source to woo into giving you information.

I stood off to the side and watched how bartenders talked to their regulars, how the more experienced reporters greeted their closest contacts, and I took meticulous notes. Mimicry is more than a form of flattery; it's a skill for survival. And I learned more by watching than I probably ever could have in a class.

Ask for help when you need it. Learn how to ask for help when you need it. The fear of looking dumb is not greater than the fear of doing something dumb that embarrasses you and jeopardizes your position. Find someone you trust, and ask for their help, whether it's looking over an e-mail before you send it to your boss, helping manage your workload, or figuring out how to ask for a raise or if you make a fair salary for your position and experience. Each new job I started, whether waitressing or reporting, was a mysterious puzzle that I had no idea how to solve. I was mortified to admit that I had no idea how to steam milk or get a source to talk on the record, but I very quickly realized that putting my ego into a box, locking it, and storing it somewhere out of sight was the best way to pick up new abilities and traits.

Learn how to work (well) with others. Most of the places I waitressed pooled tips, which we split at the end of the night. It made the work environment much more collegial, even though we liked to compete to see who had the highest sales and got the biggest tips before they went into a communal pot to be divided among us and our support staff of bussers and dishwashers. But you quickly realized that if one person was having a spectacularly rough evening, it was going to affect the smoothness of your night, as well as how much money you'd take home at the end of your shift. So you learned fairly swiftly to keep an eye on your colleagues as well as your tables, to make sure that everyone was happy and functioning and to offer up a hand when you saw that it was needed. I've brought most of that sensibility over to my jobs and experiences in the writing world because I like the culture it creates and strongly believe that there's always enough story to go around. There's much to be gained by being collaborative and supporting those around you as much as possible. Remembering that has always served me well, when I think about helping out colleagues with information, helpful links, or tidbits that I've overheard. It's a variation on the Golden Rule, which sometimes has backfired among a few rare types who took advantage of generosity but has mostly been repaid in kind.

Hustle and go. I spent the first year (or two) after college in party mode. I was thrilled to be free from classes, the rigor of academia, and the high-stress and competitive pressure that was very much a part of my undergraduate experience. I wanted to hang out, have fun, stay out late, drink cheap coffee in diners, read books, and do as little work as possible. It was glorious. I gave myself a cutoff—I would allow myself two years after college to intern and experiment with little pressure, so that I could try to figure out the path that made the most sense to me.

I cared more about figuring out my place in the world than adding lines to my résumé. Talking to many of my friends who had taken office jobs back East reinforced my decision. They were spending their days xeroxing papers and filling out spreadsheets, while I was going to lectures, reading books, and traveling when I had a little extra money to spare. I felt like I was figuring out how to be an adult, instead of just going through the motions in a desk job. I knew, even then, that it was a luxury and likely one that wouldn't last. But I gave myself a deadline. I told myself that if I didn't have something resembling a promising career by the time I was twenty-three, I'd reconsider my options and maybe even consider moving home. But the longer I stayed out in California, the more my priorities started to shift. I realized I cared less about a prestigious-sounding job and more about a happier life, full of intellectually curious people and ideas, and I started to build a world that reflected that. It was scary, turning away from the environments and traditional trajectories of my peers and family, but I trusted that my time out West wasn't going to be wild enough to permanently lead me awry, and it mostly turned out to be true. After about a year, I got bored and started to apply for internships, none of which paid, of course. So I started interning during the day, from about nine until five, jumping into a cab to my restaurant, where I would hurriedly change in the bathroom, then wait tables until midnight or so, and do it all over again the next day. For years, I had two full-time jobs, both equally demanding and unforgiving of my other obligations. I remember getting scolded by one of my intern managers for always leaving a little early. I explained to him that after I wrapped up my day job, I had to work most nights and weekends to cover my living expenses. He was sympathetic, but not really, since most of the other interns in our group didn't have to leave early. Most of them had resources from a partner or parents to help them cover their costs. But I didn't let that deter me—by that point, I had realized that I wanted to work as a writer and figuring out how to do that was my primary goal. So I didn't mind doubling up on jobs to get there. I felt good and happy knowing that I was putting in the work to make something happen. Whatever that something was, was beyond my control, but there was no lack of effort on my part. I also knew it wouldn't be forever—either it would work out and I'd start getting paid to write, or I'd switch gears and do something else. But being willing to work hard and do any job that was offered, just for the experience, helped me collect references and get known among a tiny circle of people who recommended me for other odd jobs. The fear of failure still woke me up at night, the fear of falling behind my peers still gripped me when

I browsed Facebook or e-mailed with my college friends, but I was also starting to see the first seedlings of the social web take root. Twitter and Facebook were growing in size, and I knew more about them than anything else I'd studied in college. I'd forked over my hard-earned cash for an iPhone, watched YouTube videos on how people hacked them, and tried it myself. I started to observe the way people were using those services and decided to say yes to the things that interested me—cool new things, technologies, really— that were emerging and the communities of inventive people who were experimenting with those sites and services. It's not something I would have had time to explore if I'd had a traditional nine-to-five. Even if the prospect of not having a regular postcollege job or internship was unsettling, the feeling that I was digging into a world that interested me in a way nothing else had previously was enough to sustain that momentum. I began to meet other writers and artists who worked in the service industry like me and painted or wrote during the day. I saw how it was done and I began to do it myself. I spent some time working at a Bay Area society magazine, helping to identify dilettantes and the offspring of famous local families in party pictures. I covered small parties for a city blog and sent in painstakingly written pitches to my favorite magazine at the time, *Bust* magazine. I wrote small blurbs for a free magazine called *Todo* that was based in San Francisco. I fact-checked issues of *Yoga Journal* even though I knew nothing about the practice at the time. I ghostwrote a few chapters of a travel book to Costa Rica for a travel writer who was short on time and needed a hand. I interned at a now-shuttered lesbian magazine called *Girlfriends*, even though I lived with my boyfriend. We traveled to the Dinah Shore music festival where I manned the *Girlfriends* booth, went to parties, and socialized, trying to promote our magazine. I did anything people asked me to, even if it didn't pay. I just wanted as many clips and references as I could get and didn't worry about the kinds of pieces I thought I should be writing or jobs I should be getting. Those kinds of expectations didn't make sense to me, as a total beginner and novice to writing and journalism. That willingness, I think, helped me do away with an ego that cares about the kind of work I thought I "should" be doing and taught me the value of being well-rounded and visible, both to future editors who could assign me pieces and readers who began to recognize my name.

Leave your assumptions at the door. I learned quickly not to underestimate the people I worked with or the people I served, which, by proxy, slowly ingrained in me the value of not underestimating myself. I had plenty of regulars at the Americana restaurant I worked at in Hayes Valley, but none that I liked as much as the scientists who came in on weekdays for early dinners. They were always polite and kind and never rude like so many people can be to waitstaff. They were all in their forties, perhaps, and told me they worked at NASA. They liked to test each other with space trivia and tell me random facts about planets and satellites that were currently in orbit. One day, while I was refilling their water, I listened to them talk about the Cassini mission to Saturn. I had just written a short blog post for *Wired* on radio emissions that some of the satellite's probes had picked up, and I was curious about their conversation. One of the scientists noticed my interest, and we chatted about space exploration briefly. Then he asked me a question that has stuck with me, even to this day. He said something like, "So what else do you do?" And I remember being so impressed and flattered that he seemed to genuinely want to know and that he didn't have any assumptions about who I was and understood that I had a life beyond what he could see. That interaction has stayed with me through the years and shaped the way I talk to and interact with people and the perspective I bring to the table anytime I meet someone new—not to underestimate anyone, even for a second, to recognize that your next big idea, story, friend, boss, or scoop could come from where you least expect it. The service industry isn't an easy one. It wears you down physically—most evenings, I came home, slipped off my shoes, and sank into my couch, my entire back frozen with pain, where I remained until, little by little, it loosened up enough so that I could move again. I was twenty-one, twenty-two at the time. And then there's the way it wears you down emotionally. People (usually terrible ones) talk down to you, snapping when you aren't fast enough or linger too long at their table, refuse to make eye contact, and generally treat you with little respect or view you as ambition-less, or not having a "real" career. Nearly everyone I met waitressing was in school, starting a business, writing a book, working as an artist or filmmaker, freelancing like me, or had some other side hustle or endgame that fed their creative and ambitious sides, and it was inspiring to be around other people who were grinding as hard as I was to get somewhere different in the future. I was learning how to be comfortable with my own current situation and happy to be able to support myself postcollege, something that many of my friends who were interning at law offices and in medical school still had yet to do. I didn't feel the need to explain to them about my future goals, the classes I was taking, and internships I held during the day. But that night, at that table with the kindly scientists, I felt especially vindicated and reminded to pay that kindness and respect forward as much as I could in the years ahead.

But the most important lesson of all:

Learn how to figure things out on the fly, in the moment, and don't second-guess yourself. Because sometimes you just have to get things done.

One rare too-warm day in San Francisco, I was working at a spot in Hayes Valley. We were just hitting our stride. The restaurant was at capacity, everyone was doing the unchoreographed dance known to those who work in tight quarters and have to learn to be mindful of other people's bodies at all times to avoid knocking them in the head with a hot plate or spilling a tray of drinks on a colleague who is trying to get something from behind them. We were at our peak when suddenly the lights went out. But it was more than just the lights—the power to the entire restaurant. Everything, from the credit card machines to the lights to our screen with the list of reservations on it, was down. It could have been a nightmare, but someone—probably one of the owners, who was in the kitchen where he was trying to assess the contents in the freezers—yelled, "Figure it out!" And so we did. We opened the windows and doors to let the sunlight in, someone rigged up an iPod and portable speaker system for music, and we somehow managed to end the night on a good note. Remembering moments like that, when we were faced with an impossible task but didn't melt down and instead figured out a way to solve the problem, has come in handy again and again throughout my career as a writer and a journalist, especially the very first week I walked into the *New York Times* newsrooms—no traditional experience or degree, just the confidence that I could handle anything thrown my way, because I'd done it before and pulled it off. No one's ever going to hand you a guidebook to tell you how to navigate your career or your life. Sometimes you just have to learn how to figure it the hell out yourself.

4.
WILL THE LADY IN THE BUBBLE PLEASE LET THE CAT OUT OF THE BAG?

Ruth Ann Harnisch

This used to drive me nuts about *The Wizard of Oz*. After the fire-throwing and flying-monkeys attacks, Glinda, The Good Witch, comes floating along in her pretty bubble and spills the secret of the ruby slippers. Dorothy learns she has always had the power to get what she wants, and has had it the whole time.

DOROTHY. I have?
SCARECROW. Then why didn't you tell her before?
GLINDA. Because she wouldn't have believed me. She had to learn it for herself.

Wait, what? Glinda held out? This is the *good* witch? Yes, Glinda sent poor little Dorothy careening through endless terrors and near-death experiences, then breezily announced that a simple heel-click and a few words would produce Dorothy's heart's desire. Just like that. I thought Glinda was just plain mean not to give the kid an option before scooting her on down the road.

Perhaps this is why, when any of the thousands of people I've coached ask if I know any shortcuts, I don't use Glinda's "she had to learn it for herself" method. I flat-out tell them.

And I tell them because I wish somebody had told *me*. As I write this, my life looks like the "Happily Ever After" part of the Cinderella story. But that came after a rough start in which I dropped out of college and became the third wife of my first husband. His cancer challenged us, and his addictions bankrupted us. Despite these ankle weights, I managed to have a barrier-breaking career in media. I was among the first wave of local television anchorwomen and radio talk show hosts. I was a feisty feminista in the buckle of the Bible Belt, the token progressive columnist for the conservative afternoon newspaper.

Then I married the handsome prince (in modern terms a "money manager") and my story changed. I learned that big castles and big kingdoms come with big problems, and lo! I learned that problems are usually solvable, and the solution usually starts with something simple.

Now, people come to me for help in dealing with their complex situations. They find themselves on a road fraught with flying monkeys and assorted witches. They may not dare to say it, but they hope I have some kind of magic wand.

It Can Be Easy
Clients come to me for speech coaching, fund-raising strategies, or to work on a relationship, but deep down most of them really want help removing the obstacles that keep them from enjoying their lives. At some point in our conversation, I bring out the fairy dust. This is the magic they were hoping for. I ask, "Would it be OK with you if this were easy?" The answer is usually silence.

Surprise! Many high achievers are not willing for *anything* to be easy at first. Like danger junkies who have to feel death breathing down their necks in order to feel fully alive, some people have to work doggedly for what they have in order to experience fulfillment and satisfaction. If they don't earn it the hard way, they don't feel they deserve it, or they think it was too cheaply won. Either way, they don't like it. The harder it is, the better it feels.

When we first meet, many of my clients seem to be trying to earn a life merit badge for being superbusy. I know! I spent decades believing "crazy busy" equals essential, important, working at capacity. That in-demand feeling became validation, affirmation, food for ego and soul (and wallet). I was hooked.

Clients tell me they are hardwired or were raised this way, and I was, too. A few years ago, a health scare forced me to rethink the inescapability of our programming. I finally got it, *really got it*, that my packed calendar, endless to-do list, and perennial sleep deficit had become a matter of life and death. What really terrified me was not death, but the thought of suffering a severe stroke that would leave me at the mercy of diaper-changers.

Feeling overwhelmed, fearful, and exhausted is not a price you must pay in exchange for happiness. It can be easy, if you are open to it. I can take it easy because my "No, thank you" is rock-hard.

You may have noticed that the most irresistible opportunities show up at the most inopportune times. My clients ask, "How can I say no?" Unless you work out that "No, thank you" muscle, it won't be strong enough when you need it most.

I had a chance to use my "No, thank you" muscle when I was offered the opportunity to be a guest curator of the TED conference bookstore. I looked at the e-mail again. Me? Really? What an honor! Before I could blush, I saw the deadline for choosing books to recommend. I knew that I did not have time to do a good job unless I lost sleep or shortchanged other commitments. I declined immediately. I chose "easy." And it was an easy decision.

Can you make your life easier by saying a firm and grateful "No, thank you," refusing to take on more pressure, more deadlines, more work hours, more distractions, more dilution of your energy and focus? If you can't bring yourself to say a firm no, would "Not no, but not now" work? Or must you make it hard by taking on more?

If it's OK with you for this to be easy, ask yourself these questions:

- Considering what's most meaningful to me in life, what would help me enjoy my life more?
- Is it OK with me to put myself and my needs first? (Put on your own oxygen mask before assisting others.)
- Do I think I "should" do it, or can I find the reason I am choosing to do it?

If you make it your intention, you can indeed *ease* on down the road.

Yes, You Do Too Know

The philosopher and activist Stephen Gaskin taught me, "You can always tell what somebody really wants to do, because that's what they're doing." You're not "trying to quit smoking." You're smoking or you're not. That's the power of making a decision. Better than ruby slippers.

I used to be afraid to make decisions. I was afraid of being wrong. I didn't want to be judged, criticized, or blamed. I didn't want to disappoint, look stupid, or make a truly terrible mistake with regrettable consequences. And, sometimes, I just didn't want to acknowledge the truth, because then I might have to do something about it.

Eventually, I learned that the ability to make a swift, regret-free decision was one of the finest skills I could hone. There's no stop sign on the process of information-gathering and scenario-testing; at some point, a decision's got to be made. So ask yourself: How swiftly can I get enough information to commit to this decision, make it, evaluate it, make adjustments (amends if necessary), and move forward? Regrets are a waste of time.

Decision-making shortcut: Flip a coin. Check your gut reaction when you see the result. If you feel relief and gratitude, that's the right choice. If you feel anguish and regret, it's the wrong one. In case of emergency, go with your gut, being true to your truest self and your own values. As Stephen Gaskin says, "You do too know." (And you do.)

If It's Not One Thing, It's Your Mother

As you go through life making decisions and evaluating what comes before you, whose voice is in your head? Who is your commentator, who provides the play-by-play, who's judging you up there?

It would have been *great* to have Glinda show up early in my life with this shortcut: authority figures cannot hijack the voice in my head *without my permission*. In other words, authority figures can tell you what to believe, but they can't force you to believe it. That requires your cooperation.

One of my most frequent tasks as a coach is congratulating clients for being such good children. Their parents would be so proud! Because no matter how unhappy it makes them, they are allowing their parents' values to control their adult lives and influence their adult choices. So many people are completely unaware that they live in a soul-killing prison built of their parents' values, even after their parents are deceased.

A man contacted me after landing in the hospital, exhausted from working too many hours. He thought he wanted better organizational skills. We discovered the truth: he hated his work and didn't want to disappoint his parents by quitting. When he realized this, he saw he could make it easy. He decided that his parents would be more disappointed if he were dead. So he told them the truth, and he is living happily ever after.

There is an internationally famous figure who wept when she tried to ask me for money for her nonprofit. It took less than five minutes for her to figure out that her tears were about her late mother, who would have been ashamed. Her daughter—divorced, having to work, and asking strangers for money? When she was able to focus on her sincere passion for the nonprofit's purpose, she could explain it to her "mother," her mother's voice in her mind. She tells me now she is sure her mother would approve, and might even be helping her from beyond.

But parents aren't the only ones in command. Some hear the voice of a spouse, loving and supportive, while others hear a spouse second-guessing, judging, belittling, and criticizing. A lot of men tell me the voice in their head is a former athletic coach. Teachers, bosses, bullies—they and many others want to tell you what they think of your choices. Do you let them? Author Joyce Duco taught me to say with a smile, "What you think of me is none of my business."

Before you can take charge of your life, you have to wrestle the microphone away from whoever is your critical inner voice. If I am having negative thoughts about myself, I stop and ask, who's talking? Sometimes, with all due respect, I have to tell my (late) mother, "I've got this, Ma. Give it a rest."

You Tell Yourself the Story

For most of my life, I didn't know that humans could control their own minds. Thoughts came to me! What was I supposed to do about *that*? My brain activity seemed to unspool before me without any input from my consciousness. And then I discovered the power: I am not only the producer, writer, director, and star of the movie of my life. *I am the editor.*

I can choose what to think. I can interrupt thoughts of worry, blame, anger, selfishness, frustration, and fear. Especially fear. I can choose to replace unproductive thoughts with better ones. I can think of next steps and larger strategies. I can imagine better options, if I *choose* to. Here's what my editing process looks like:

- I halt unproductive thoughts as soon as I recognize that I'm having them—when all else fails, I sing "Happy Birthday" or whistle the theme song from *The Andy Griffith Show*. Anything to derail the unhelpful thought.
- I no longer allow myself to wander alone down dark alleys of thought. I don't want to watch gory true crime or listen to sad songs or read books on subjects bound to upset me. Real life's tough enough. Why deliberately go places where my thoughts get mugged and dragged away?
- At my worst times, I reach for the happiest thought I can think in that moment. My young nephew died suddenly in June. Happy thoughts were hard to come by, but happier ones were within reach. *Our family is here together to help each other. I will always have feelings of love when I think of him. I will treasure my own aliveness in this moment.*
- I find the strength to hang on by reaching for a thought that is even just the teensiest bit better. If I can't think of one, I ask for help. Sometimes the little-bit-happier thought is, *I can get more helpful help than that.* (And yes, sometimes help means calling in the pros. A confidante, a coach, a therapist—whatever's needed for the job at hand.)

In over forty years of talking with people as a journalist, a coach, and a friend, I've met people who made it through natural disasters, health challenges that should have been fatal, and the most heinous crimes people can survive. They survived because they would not allow their minds to stay in the dark places. Even in the midst of catastrophe, people can count their blessings and look ahead. It doesn't mean they're not heartbroken, doesn't mean life won't be challenging. It means they choose to take control of their thoughts and decide to enjoy even the fleeting moments of their lives as much as they can, while they can.

Coaches help their clients understand that life is the story you tell yourself. I remind my clients to tell themselves the happiest story that is true.

Just Stop It

Remember when the Cowardly Lion threatens Toto, and Dorothy stops him cold with a big fat slap? When my vivid imagination begins taking me to places where I feel frightened, angry, negative, or sad, I just have to slap my thought and say, "Stop it!"

You might find it hard to believe that six letters and one space can be so powerful. Those two simple words can derail the most worrisome, self-loathing, and hateful thoughts. It's not easy to shut down the screaming voice of naked fear or grief. I still have moments of darkness, times when I cannot find a ray of hope. Somehow, I have been able to ask myself, "Where's this headed? What's the emotional and physical cost of getting caught up in this cyclone of negative thought? Can I just *stop it?*"

Yes, *just stop it.* I say it as many times as I need to until I, you know, stop it. The more I do it, the easier it is. Eventually, when "Stop it!" muscles grow strong enough, clients find profound transformation seeping into all aspects of their lives, perhaps choosing a new career, ending destructive patterns, or healing unhealthy relationships. I like to follow "Stop it!" with a chaser of "Things always have a way of working out for me."

Breathe

Check it out: Are you breathing? I know, I know, if you weren't breathing you'd be dead. But if you pay attention, you might catch yourself holding your breath. I didn't realize how often I stopped breathing until my television performance coach pointed it out.

The first time somebody tried to talk to me about conscious breathing, I got the giggles so badly I had to cut to commercial. I was interviewing a rebirther, someone who works one-on-one with clients using breath. "Let me get this straight," I said. "You take money from people to breathe with them?" I lost it. I laughed so hard and so uncontrollably that even my guest joined in.

Eventually, I learned more about yoga, meditation, and bio-feedback for stress relief. I came to understand that breathing techniques are powerful tools of self-control. I learned to slow my breath, to calmly concentrate on the intake and outflow. I was a jumpy kid, a jittery adult. Breathing consciously and slowly has helped me to become less rattled in life. In circumstances where I might have allowed myself to raise my voice in anger or go into full-blown panic over the imagined end of my world, I have been able to keep myself focused without allowing my emotions and wild thoughts to take over, simply by breathing consciously and slowly.

There is nothing faster, cheaper, simpler, closer, more universally available, or easier to grab in case of emergency: breath. It's power-ful enough to keep you alive! So why not use it for other big jobs? Breathe slowly, breathe deeply, and allow the breath to calm you.

Put On Green Glasses and You're in Emerald City

Did you know that in L. Frank Baum's book, everyone who entered the Emerald City was required to put on green-tinted glasses (which is why it looked like the Emerald City)? This was before Technicolor.

It's all in how you look at things, what frame you put on the picture. When I hear myself using language of complaint, I reframe. I don't "have to" do the things I've committed to. I *get* to.

I'm alive. I'm capable. I can get around, see, and hear. I'm not in crippling pain. Subtract any one of those factors and my life would not be enjoyable in the same way it is right now, so I'm enjoying what is there to enjoy.

Have you ever had a flat tire? After the first time I had to cope with the fear, the danger, and the details of getting the tire changed (before the days of cell phones), I became a naturally cheery driver. A snarl of traffic? Stuck behind the slowest driver? Construction? It was *so much better than a flat tire*! For months I was happily mindful almost every time I turned off the ignition. *I didn't have a flat tire!* Enjoy what there is to enjoy.

When a legitimate cause for concern arises, I choose to look for solutions instead of scapegoats. Far more important than "How did I get in this mess?" is "How do I get out of it?" Try it—just because you get to.

You and Your Ideas Need a Community

My generation of middle-class United States citizens got the message that individual achievement was the measure of success. And we also learned to be *rugged* individualists—never let 'em see you sweat, big girls and boys don't cry, no thanks, no help needed, no help wanted.

While there are still some holdouts who believe success and well-being are a personal matter, that delusion has been shattered for most of us. Today's world works in collaboration—at least the smartest and happiest part of the world does.

There is no clearer distinction between old-thinkers and new-thinkers. An alliance-based approach to life marks the modern. We play video games with strangers, communicate on social networks, fund businesses and charities with a click, gather online to find friends and solutions. Ignore this reality at your peril.

For the most basic stuff in life—love, birth, illness, catastrophe, death—people need community. Wherever there is a need, the best solution is a caring circle of people whose collective strengths can make the difference. Well-tended relationships are life's greatest joy, not to mention the greatest insurance policy. We are there for each other when the chips are down. Perhaps if Glinda had made clear to me how much I was going to need help, and how much help I was capable of giving, I would have been less of a loner.

And I wouldn't have wasted so much time on projects that didn't have widespread buy-in from key stakeholders. If an idea doesn't have a community, it's not going to survive. If the idea-generator can't inspire a solid core of support to bring the idea forth, the idea stands little chance of success. Before I invest in an idea these days, I want to know if it is already resonating with a passionate core community that will be its life-support system as it grows. If something were to happen to the idea-generator, is the idea positioned to survive without that person?

Almost all of my unhappiest clients cling to an unshakable belief that they should do things for themselves, by themselves, despite being part of a healthy community of people who would be delighted to assist. Sometimes the greatest favor we can do for someone else is to allow them to help us. That's how I learned to accept—and even ask for—help. I started out by "doing them a favor" by allowing them to help because I could see that it meant a lot to them. So I let them. And it turns out that help is, well, helpful.

Learning to be a gracious receiver opens the door to unprecedented opportunities. You won't be able to enjoy them unless you can say a guilt-free "Yes, thank you!" to the offers life brings your way.

Everybody Feels Like a Fraud Sometimes

The Wizard really was a fraud! But there's a difference between a deliberate misrepresentation and a perceived gap in competence. My clients include some of the most talented and successful people I've ever known. Yet so many of them feel as if they don't deserve what they have, or aren't as good as they "should" be. They downplay their own attributes while standing in awe of people no better than they. Peek behind the curtain, and it's easy to see that all of these wizards feel—and are—only human.

Human beings are fallible by design. To be a perfect human is to make mistakes. We learn by doing, by experimenting, by seeing what works. I've learned that the happiest people are the ones who are the most authentically *themselves.* They are who they are, not trying to be anyone they're not. They are comfortable in their bodies. They are at peace with themselves. When I exhibit symptoms of Imposter Syndrome—feeling as if I don't belong where I am, that I'm not worthy of being where I am, that it will soon be obvious how much I don't deserve to be here—I do a reality check.

Sometimes I really do need to up my game: study more, have more conversations, learn new skills. Sometimes I need to get an objective opinion. Or two. Or more. And sometimes I simply need to recognize that *almost everyone I've ever had a deep conversation with about this subject admits there are times they have felt like an imposter.*

Should you "fake it 'til you make it," as some recommend? Yes, do fake an air of confidence until you can develop confidence. Yes, do fake a cheerful demeanor rather than being a sincere grouch. Yes, do fake your courage until you find it. But I beg of you, don't fake in the face of demonstrable facts. Don't fake with your spreadsheets, in meetings with your partners or your would-be investors, or on your tax returns. Don't fake your competence, thereby torpedoing the efforts of others. If you're faking the key skill sets, that's not "feeling like a fraud." That's *being* a fraud. Stop it. Bad Wizard.

People Will Disappoint You

If someone tells me I'm wonderful I say, "Thank you. And please remember that I'm going to disappoint you in some way." This is not to denigrate myself. This is to invite a clear look at reality—nobody's perfect—and to begin the relationship with honest expectations. Everyone is, as Kris Kristofferson wrote, "A walking contradiction, partly truth and partly fiction."

Some of the people who are the dearest to me have surprised me by behaving in a way I did not expect. Sometimes they broke agreements. Sometimes they did things they knew would cause me pain. When Dorothy had done everything the Wizard told her she needed to do to get where she wanted to go, surprise! He couldn't deliver.

After being disappointed by a few wizards, I learned what conditions needed to be met in order to trust someone. I learned not to trust anyone to do or be anything they haven't explicitly agreed to be trusted to do or be. I used to trust people without telling them—I had expectations that they knew nothing about, a surefire recipe for disappointment. In other words, they had to be expressly willing to be trusted.

I learned that people can't be trusted to do something they're not capable of doing. The hard part is telling myself the truth about what others are truly capable of doing (added to the first condition, willingness).

And finally, I learned to look for a proven track record of trustworthiness. I can only trust someone in proportion to the amount of time I've had to observe their trustworthiness. Maya Angelou often says, "When people show you who they are, believe them the first time." Now I pay better attention to what people's actions are telling me about who they are (especially if their actions contradict their words). That helps me decide where to place my trust.

This is not to say that I expect people to be perfect—just perfectly themselves. Anybody you think is "normal" is someone you don't know very well yet. A friend's theory: everybody's weird in their own way, and the key to happiness is to find people whose weirdness is compatible with your weirdness.

People disappoint me and I disappoint people. I get over things that should be gotten over. I work for resolution and reconciliation. If I hadn't learned to do this, I would have missed some of the most precious relationships of my life. Entering into relationships with a clear understanding that people *will* disappoint you can erase the anxiety about if and when it could happen.

I try to head off disappointment by being clear about my deal-breaking boundaries. Oh, that is one of the wish-someone-would-have-told-me basics: boundaries. Have them. Know what works for you and what doesn't. Communicate clearly about what you won't accept, and fortify your boundaries by repeatedly enforcing them.

Boundaries are as individual as fingerprints, so we have to map our own boundaries. By paying attention to our feelings, we recognize what makes us feel threatened or unsafe. That's how we learn to establish and enforce our personal boundaries. Where do you draw the line with your family members, friends, colleagues?

Yes, those dearest to us do occasionally lack courage, heart, or brains (and that's true of me, too), but linking arms with these companions and setting off on the yellow brick road is what makes life's adventures worthwhile.

Everybody Dies and You Will, Too

"My! People come and go so quickly here!" said Dorothy. Here, too.

I was in television news for over a decade. You can imagine how many deaths I had to report. Day after day, death after death, the message was inevitable. I am going to die, and everyone I know is going to die. Relatively few of us get enough notice to write the final script.

When people face the facts of death, the result can be a mighty passion for life. I've been devastated by the sudden death of a beloved young nephew. Tagging along at the heels of my sadness is a tiny sparkle of inspiration, reminding me to get on with whatever I want to accomplish while I still can.

Sometimes a coaching relationship is "'til death us do part." When a client I'm coaching on leadership skills develops a life-threatening illness, I can—and have—coached to death. The philanthropist Tracy Gary urges people to act now on their best intentions. "Tick tock," she says, tapping her wrist where a watch would have been in another century. She quotes the poet Mary Oliver: "Tell me, what is it you plan to do / with your one wild and precious life?"

I often do a reality check and ask myself, "Is this what you'd be doing if you knew you only had a week (or a month, or a year) to live?" I try to remember that there will be a last time for everything. I will see people for the last time, and I probably won't know it when it's happening. So I try never to leave my loved ones with anything less than the quality of affection I would want to express if I knew it was the last time. Because one time it will be.

Be Kind to Yourself

It would sound particularly saccharine coming from a blonde with a wand and a trilling voice, so if Glinda had told me one of the secrets of enjoying life was to be kind, I might have gagged. But that was before I learned to recognize kindness.

The kindness of others had carried me without my knowing, until I had such troubles that I couldn't help seeing that kindness was a form of pain relief unlike any other. Score one for "She had to learn it for herself." The Dalai Lama says that kindness *is* his religion, all wrapped up in a single word, and I now know, intimately, that the kindness of other people is a bit of padding against the sharp edges of life.

We have no idea of the secret suffering all around us. Almost everyone can use a little kindness, and I am mindful that gossiping or making jokes at someone else's expense is not kind. In my youth, it was a badge of honor to deliver a sharply cutting remark, and that's still valuable currency in many circles. I worked in newsrooms for most of my career. Hi, my name is Ruth Ann, and I'm a recovering snarkaholic.

I'm also recovering from seeing the world in black and white, right or wrong. This has required me to resign from the Supreme Court. Oh, you didn't know I was the judge of everything? I used to be great at judging others, and I did my best work judging myself.

In her autobiography, actress Kitty Carlisle wrote about a daily ritual that was a secret of her serenity and joy. She looked at herself in the mirror every day and said, "I forgive you, Kitty." When I first read that, I was unable to wrap my head around the concept of self-forgiveness. Forgiveness was a concept I had not yet learned. (See "If It's Not One Thing, It's Your Mother.")

I told my sister about Kitty's ritual. She was as disbelieving, and aghast, as I was. (Same mother.) "Could you ever do that? Could you say that to yourself?" my sister asked incredulously. "No, I can't," I said. "I tried and I couldn't do it. So instead I say, 'I forgive you, Kitty.'" We still laugh about that. And sometimes I still say, "I forgive you, Kitty," while looking into my own eyes. Every time I do it, I'm amazed at how good it feels. When I learned to forgive myself for not being perfect, it was easier to forgive everyone else for not being perfect.

Now I stop my clients from speaking unkindly of themselves. "I'm so stupid!" "I'm so clumsy!" or "I'm so bad at that!" I interrupt their self-blaming rants, telling them I don't let *anybody* talk about my client like that, not even my client.

Defend yourself at least as well as you would fight for someone you actually loved, such as your closest friends, your dearest kin, and your little dog, too.

Your Life Is Up to You

If Glinda had told me that my life was my responsibility, I would have argued with her. How could whatever is going wrong be my fault? It was obvious that there were plenty of other people to blame for everything wrong in my life, from the dent in my car door to the failure of my million-dollar investment. I could name them all for you now, except . . . the only person who made the choices was me.

Sure, I had collaborators, instigators, and antagonists. There were circumstances! There were reasons! And in the end there are no excuses. The first rule of relationships: the only person in the relationship you can change is yourself.

As it turns out, that's true about my relationship with life and everyone and everything in it. Not only am I the only one I can change, but I'm the only one who can change myself.

Whenever I think someone else is to blame for something going on in my life, I use author Byron Katie's suggestion to substitute my name for the other person's name, and consider what truth emerges if I turn the statement around. "My husband is making me crazy!" becomes "I am making me crazy!" or "I am making my husband crazy!" or "My husband is making me sane!" "She should not have done that" becomes "She should have done that," or "I should not have done that," or "I should have done that."

It might take a few minutes (or years) to figure out why the reverse statement has truth, but I eventually recognize why I am accountable to myself for the situation. When I'm in disagreement with someone, I've learned to make "I" statements ("I feel so angry right now!") instead of "You" statements ("You make me so mad!") because I need to take responsibility for the story I'm telling. What other people say or do shouldn't matter because the only thing I can control is my reaction to what happens. "I" statements acknowledge that my life is up to me, not some outsider.

If I'd been able to recognize how responsible I was for my part of everything I was unhappy about, I could have taken ownership of my problems and tried to solve them. Instead, I was under the illusion that my unhappiness was somebody else's fault, starting with my parents and eventually widening the net to include everyone on the planet. Shout-out to some extra-hateful teachers, a couple of heartbreaking exes, and the bosses who know who they are. If Glinda had said, "You are responsible for *how you react* to everything that happens," I wonder if I still would have had to learn it for myself.

Still Waiting for Your Answers to Come from the Sky?
The witches and the flying monkeys never stop coming at you. There are no original weapons against them here; you have heard *all* of this before. If you're stuck, help is somewhere. Keep looking. It's probably something simple, the "*Now* you tell me" truth that's always a bit too late but somehow right on time. And just like with those ruby slippers, the action doesn't start until you click your heels and say the words. There's no time like now . . . there's no time like now . . .

5.
CONTROLLED BURN

Paula Froelich

A prescribed or controlled burn is a purposely set, regulated fire used to rejuvenate open areas to create lush and healthy grasslands. Contrary to popular myth, fire actually helps many open land wildlife species. Burning stimulates new grass growth and retards the growth of brush and trees, which can overtake open areas and crowd out some animal and plant species.
—*The Benefits of Prescribed Burning on Private Land*, The Minnesota Department of Natural Resources, Section of Wildlife.

Hello, I'm Paula Froelich. Doesn't ring a bell? But I'm familiar somehow . . . You've seen me somewhere before but just can't place it, right? Right? Maybe you didn't hear me the first time: I'm Paula Froelich. Still nothing? Maybe you are unaware that I used to be *kind of a big deal.* I don't want to embarrass you or anything, but I did write the *New York Times* bestselling novel *Mercury in Retrograde*, edited a national gossip column for almost a decade, and appeared on your TV every night yammering about the foibles of the rich and famous for many of those years. If you don't believe me—you can Google me.[1]

By the standards outlined in the *Froelich Family Guide to Life* (an oral manual), I had not only been successful, but I had *made it*. I had a seat at almost every dinner party in town, photographers took my picture on many a red carpet, and I made enough money to be able to buy my mother's house, so she didn't have to deal with a mortgage. I hung out with a group of other successful women and our exploits were featured in newspapers, magazines, and websites. Hell, I was so successful that when I was thirty, I even wrote a book about how to be successful.[2]

Even though this is a series on successful women and their success secrets, this essay is different. This is not your typical "How to Be a Raging Runaway Star" story, or, not unlike one of my previous books, a stairway to riches and fame story written by a naïve yet arrogant thirty-year-old who needed to pay off her student loans. This is a story about how, at the apex of my career, I had to blow up my life and set a "controlled burn" to learn what real success was.

---

1. Okay, listen, I swear that's me. I just look a little different now. I used to have straight(ened) blonde hair and wear a ton of makeup that would rival any *RuPaul's Drag Race* contestant. In my defense, looking like a cracked out transvestite wasn't really my preference—for TV they have makeup artists available to on-air talent, and they really spackle the stuff on an inch thick. It's like a rule. Kind of like wearing clothes in block "TV-friendly colors." You know, the hot pinks, greens, teals, and blues that morning-show hosts wear to help them "pop" on camera and complement their overly caffeinated smiles.

2. *It! Nine Secrets of the Rich and Famous That Will Take You to the Top.* Available online!

Part I: The Curse of the Dancing Monkey

At the risk of sounding like Patty Duke, there are two things I must address—both of which live in my head and are not visible to the naked eye. I'm not too embarrassed by this as, after having a few in-depth conversations with other people, I'd wager one or both of them live in your head as well. Let me first introduce you to Rhonda. Rhonda is that bitch who hangs out in my subconscious,[3] smoking cigarettes, drinking moonshine, and saying all those vicious things nobody ever wants to hear. You know, things like, *Who the hell do you think you are? You're not good enough . . . You're not smart enough . . . You didn't go to the right school . . . You don't fit in . . . You're a fraud . . . Your nose is too big . . . Your thighs are too fat . . . You can slap some lipstick on a pig, but it's still a pig . . . No one will ever love you . . . Sorry kid, things just aren't meant to work out for you. You're not one of the lucky ones . . . Don't worry—people will catch on soon to who you really are and fire your ass . . . Things may be going good right now but wait for it—the other shoe is gonna fall and it's gonna fall hard.*

You know. *That* voice. For me, it was an amalgam of my mother's and father's voices, and whispers of every setback and insecurity I'd ever had—a result of growing up with an absentee religious father, a pessimistic mother, frizzy hair, and a unibrow in a lower middle–class home in Ohio.[4]

Now let's be clear. In, say, 2003, most people would've never known Rhonda was in there, whispering those vile words in my ear at all times. Most people saw what I wanted them to see—a manicured woman with straight blonde hair who'd finally learned how to properly work a pair of tweezers. I dressed impeccably in very expensive clothes, worked at a very powerful gossip column,

---

3. Uninvited, I might add!
4. Where the standards of beauty were set by Farrah Fawcett. Not Darlene from *Roseanne*.

and was on TV for Christ's sake. People even recognized me in the street. In Ohio! But, perhaps because I was in the limelight and had reached a level of success no one else in my family ever had, Rhonda became louder. I had faked it till I made it—but learned a little too late that when you make it based on an inherent belief that you are a fake, shit can really (internally) hit the fan.

Enter the Monkey.

The Monkey, ironically, was born out of all the insecurities Rhonda whispered about. I say *ironically* because if you're not looking too closely, when I'm in Monkey mode, I appear the most confident, the brashest, the funniest, smartest girl in the room— like the proverbial dancing monkey performing for the crowds. But the Monkey is made up of everything I fear. I'm not pretty enough? Okay, I'll be funny! I'm not good enough? Look, I'm smart! I'm in the know—I know everything about everyone and can tell a story like no one else!

The Monkey was a hell of a good time and got me a seat at many a dinner table. I was, after all, the entertainment.

But the Monkey had a dark side with no boundaries. It could turn the corner from smart to sarcastic, from funny to caustic, in the blink of an eye. Although the Monkey was there to counterbalance Rhonda, they were really two sides of the same insecure coin. When Rhonda got louder, the Monkey danced harder—until the whole tango became macabre.

By early 2009, the Monkey had taken over my life. It had become out of control and feral. Somewhere in my head, Rhonda was whispering *I told you so*.

Several things had happened to cause this, starting with The Disaster of 2006. The year started off well. I was happy(ish) at the gossip column, working with people whom I not only loved but who actually made me feel smarter for interacting with them. My two full-time coworkers felt like family, as at no point in my life had I ever spent as much time with two people. Ever. We worked eight- to ten-hour days together in the office, then oftentimes spent several hours with each other at night. For a girl whose mother had once worked four jobs at a time, this was a lot of bonding. I was also a correspondent at a daily entertainment show on network TV, earning an obscene amount of money for a five-second spot every day in which I would utter inanities like, "Lindsay Lohan was spotted wearing a polka-dot dress, Ray-Bans, and a fedora walking out of the Maritime Hotel on her way to the airport while talking on her cell phone to the new love of her life." Or stand in line on a red carpet vying to ask silicone-enhanced celebrities such life-changing questions as, "Who made your dress?" "What was it like working with Robert De Niro?" or "Are you dating anyone?"

And then came The Disaster, heralding the dawn of what I like to call The Angry Era. In April of 2006, a freelancer for the column I worked on was caught extorting a billionaire. The ensuing media frenzy was a nightmare. Turns out some of my coworkers had accepted extravagant gifts and cash. All freelancers were immediately fired, my closest coworker quit, and my boss became paranoid, aloof, and retaliatory. The TV show, not wanting to be identified with the scandal, ended my contract and the majority of my income. Because I hadn't been caught up in the scandal, I had to carry the heavy load of the column alone. My boss went away for a few months on what amounted to a sabbatical, and I was left with a junior staffer and a rewrite guy to fill three pages of news every day. My work family was replaced by two self-identifying misogynists, one of whom took to playing loud barnyard animal noises on his computer every time I spoke, while the other refused to talk to me at all except to make porn references, accompanied by "rape is funny" jokes.[5] When I voiced my unhappiness to management, I was told

5. These are, in fact, to those who might not know, the exact opposite of funny. Nor is date rape—as it was also asserted—a "fake" crime

to "stop acting like a child and get back to work," that I couldn't quit because "it would look like you were hiding something"—and then I was punished in a variety of inventive ways.

Added to the *mishegoss* at work, was my personal life. My mother and I were fighting all the time, and my father and I, after years of not speaking, were trying to find common ground. Seeing as my dad is a right-wing, born-again, gun-collecting tea partier, prone to thinking most people (including his technically Jewish daughter) were going to hell—this was not an easy journey.

The continued stress at work, a lack of a viable support system at home, and the strain of keeping up appearances[6] led to a burgeoning, relentless depression and an almost complete physical breakdown. I stopped sleeping at night and started taking hours-long naps under my desk at work like a crazy, homeless lady. I began having panic attacks, and my health suffered. By May 2009, within a single year I'd had three bouts of influenza, four trips to the doctor for bronchitis, and a nine-month-long incurable yeast infection due to a "severely compromised immune system." Two out of three doctors advised me to quit my job and even slipped me numbers of other professionals—who just happened to be employment lawyers.[7]

If I'm honest with myself, and these days I try hard to be, even before The Disaster, I'd been unsatisfied. I'd happened upon the job at the gossip column accidentally and had never harbored any dreams

---

in which "the chick is just pissed because the guy didn't call her the next day."

6. Because in the annals of "fake it till you make it," one must always keep up appearances. And no one ever looked too closely, so they never saw the inch of makeup hiding the bags under my eyes or that my smile had become strained. It's a thin line between excited and ghoulish, and very few can tell the difference in low light.

7. Talk about networking!

of being the next Cindy Adams, Liz Smith, or Richard Johnson. By 2006, I was bored and felt like I was starring in a demented version of *Groundhog Day*. And while the TV job paid well, I balked at it intellectually. When I was told I was set to become the next full-time correspondent (and thereby double my already insane paycheck), I became depressed instead of joyful—wondering to myself, *Is this really what I'm supposed to be doing with my life?*

In hindsight, I can only think that while The Disaster sucked, it was the much-needed catalyst to release me from a career I'd become identified with but didn't really want and was too wimpy to leave. And it's not like my behavior was stellar during The Angry Era (2006–2009). As I got more stressed, the feral Monkey took over. I dated the wrong men, became friends with the wrong people while treating the right people horribly, and wielded the pseudo-righteous stick from the bully pulpit of the gossip column. I wrote in judgment, without compassion and, to feed the beast, sometimes without all the facts—because I'd already made up my mind. I'd turned into a *bitch*. A mean, vicious, self-righteous, miserable bitch.

And so, four years ago, I did the unthinkable. I pulled the rip cord and methodically set about burning down the "successful" life that I'd built under false pretenses—so that another, more fruitful, honest one could take its place. I started by doing what most New Yorkers do when things get weird—I went on meds and saw a shrink, whom I called The Stang. After one session, The Stang looked at me and said, "I'm here to re-parent you. To teach you how to self-soothe and be a functioning adult—and to stop being a permanent adolescent."

Part II: The Burn
On July 25, 2009, at 3:24 p.m., two weeks after my novel had hit the *New York Times* bestseller list, I put on Johnny Paycheck's "Take

This Job and Shove It" on my work computer, said good-bye to the newsroom, and walked out of the job I'd held for ten years.

But I wasn't stupid. It wasn't a case of just losing it one day and screaming "EFF THIS. I'M OUT!" (Although, trust me, the thought crossed my mind on a regular basis.) In a way, Rhonda saved me. Because of all her daily repeated fears (of being broke, of being homeless, of ending up back in Ohio), I'd come up with a plan. Because I'd been so unhappy for so long, I knew I'd need money to leave my job without another one waiting in the wings. I also knew I was in no position, mentally or physically, to jump from one job to another—especially when I had no idea what I wanted to do. So, starting in 2007, I stopped all frivolous spending and started stockpiling cash. Then, in 2008, I sold the proposal for *Mercury in Retrograde*, wrote it quickly, and timed my departure for a month after it hit the shelves. I figured (rightly) that no one could say anything if I left to become a novelist. It was respectable and had been done before by Jeannette Walls, who'd left her position as a gossip columnist for msnbc.com after the runaway success of her memoir, *The Glass Castle*.

I set the spark two years before the fire publicly burned. But walking out was the easy part.

I went home and unpacked some boxes from the office. A week later, I'd fielded hundreds of e-mails, phone calls, and text messages, mostly from people who wanted to know WHAT WAS I THINKING? How could I quit such a powerful, fun, amazing dream job? Or, what was the "real story" on why I'd left? What was I doing next? Some people had heard I was moving to Los Angeles (I was not), others wanted to know how many people had "dropped" me after I quit.[8] After I cleaned out my e-mail in-boxes, deleted my

---

8. I know! So crazy! Creepily enough, they were even kind of gleeful about it. I was like, "Hell, my seat ain't even cold yet, and you're

phone messages, and ignored the texts, I sat there. Alone. Something I hadn't truly allowed myself to be for over a decade.[9]

After I woke up from the two-week nap I'd embarked upon, I quickly realized a few things:

- The stove in the apartment I'd lived in for six years (which, up until then, had been used for storage), didn't actually work.
- There were a lot of hours in the day to fill.
- Those hours were made up of very long minutes.
- Those minutes were filled with crippling anxiety (*What was I going to do with the rest of my life? Would I be able to make a living? Was I a hack writer? Had my book only hit the bestseller list because I had shoved it onto every media platform available to me? Did it really suck? Did I suck? Would I go broke and end up back in Ohio? Who was I if I was Paula Froelich the Unemployed?*). There was a deep sense of grief and loss (Had I just wasted years of my life?), and bizarrely, I felt like a death had occurred.
- I was terrified to leave my house.

This last realization was especially odd for me. In my previous existence, I'd used my house only as a place to sleep, bathe, and change clothes. I'd eaten out for breakfast, lunch, and dinner for a decade, and had been constantly surrounded by other people and distractions. Now all I wanted to do was stay inside my apartment—so much so, I started to feel like it was a prison. But still, I couldn't leave. On particularly bad days when Rhonda was exceptionally loud, I developed a system called "hiding"—wherein I'd

wondering who dropped me?" But that's how people think sometimes.

9. And by "alone" I mean with only Karl Froelich, the canine unicorn, for company.

grab my iPad and a blanket, go in my closet, and shut the door. "Hiding Lite" involved just going under the bed covers with my computer for the day. If it weren't for Karl[10] and The Stang, I might not have ventured onto or off of Sullivan Street for months. Possibly years.

Making things worse was the dawning realization that many of the people I had surrounded myself with, including people I once considered close friends, were a little noxious. I had friends (and family members) who, after eating and drinking for free on either my expense account or personal tab for years, never bought me a drink when I left my job and had no income coming in. Yet they would still want to hang out—and still forget to bring their wallets. There were people for whom I had helped find apartments, jobs, and even husbands, who, once they were in a position to aid me, didn't. I started to notice I had friends who, during the course of an entire evening, never asked me how I was doing—or if they did, didn't wait for the answer. There were even people (plural!) who I clocked in at talking nonstop, using circular breathing, about themselves for over an hour before making their excuses and leaving—without even a "How's your new unemployed life going? You changed your sheets yet?" But by far the most troubling for me was a dawning realization that these people didn't think or expect the best of me and only saw a debased version of me. When I made a mistake, as humans do, they were unforgiving. They were supportive to my face, but talked behind my back. They were unsupportive of me changing anything internally at all. They basically treated me the way I had treated myself for years. And, again, if I'm honest, they were behaving as I had behaved. How many times had I controlled and dominated a conversation without a care for whatever anyone else was going through? How many times had I asked (and really cared) about how someone else was doing? How many times

10. The aforementioned canine unicorn.

had I held an often inane grudge—for years? How many times had I judged someone and thought the worst of them without ever giving them a chance to explain? Most of the people I had surrounded myself with during The Angry Era were the living embodiments of Rhonda and the Monkey.

In retrospect, it was quite easy to flush them out. I either stopped e-mailing, calling, paying the tab,[11] or I simply refused to leave a two-block radius of my house.[12] If we did meet up, I'd explain I was trying out some new habits, which on face value were met with "oh cool," but in practice, the response felt more like "fuck you." The first time I had to tell someone *in a loving way* that she had upset me and was doing some things that were hurtful, I started crying.[13] I'm not kidding. I was so not used to peaceful, loving confrontation that my entire body rejected it. I was inured to a black-and-white world—you did right till you messed up, and then you were out. Apologies meant nothing. There were no shades of gray.

---

11. Or, explaining that I couldn't afford to hang out with them anymore if they didn't pay their full share. Funny how, after I'd stopped footing the whole bill, they would still show up, but with very little money—using the old "I forgot to go to the ATM" or "Oops, I only have ten dollars with me" excuse. You know, *those* people.

12. Not because—as they claimed behind my back, naturally—I was self-obsessed and liked to manipulate people to come to me, but because, for a hot minute there, I literally couldn't wrap my head around leaving a two-block radius. Going above Houston Street gave me palpitations. I started to sweat if I went past Bleecker, and don't get me started on what happened if I even thought about walking past West Fourth.

13. Normal ways of dealing with someone who hurt your feelings: roll your eyes, bottle it up, bitch behind their back and then, at some later date, explode.

Now, don't cry (too hard) for me, Argentina. There were plenty of wonderful people in my life who were supportive, caring, and had always seen my awesomeness even when I wasn't aware I had any at all. They let out a collective THANK GOD sigh of relief when I started to turn my ship around. They also gave me room to do so. Room I needed because, as insane as it sounds, I had to learn how to behave again. I had to admit to wrongdoing. To learn how to apologize. To learn how to be a human being I was proud of. To learn how to be honest with myself.

More than anything, I had to learn how to trust myself.

And some things you can only do on your own. In unfamiliar surroundings.

And so, because I couldn't leave my house, I left the country.

Part III: Sowing the Field
Oddly enough, while I couldn't leave a two-block radius of my apartment, I found I could pack a bag and fly four thousand miles away.

During those days of hiding in my closet or under my comforter, I thought of my childhood dream of traveling the world and exploring foreign lands. During the dark days at the column, I would fantasize about being anywhere but there—and that anywhere usually involved a camel ride. I was reminded of how brave I used to be. How, after college, I moved to London for two years and then went to India, Nepal, and Thailand for six months with only $1500 in my pocket. I remember being so intimidated of going to London or India (which in 1997 was very rustic and not high on anyone's travel list) that I put it off for months, thinking, *I can't do this.* When I finally did it, I was furious with myself for not doing it sooner because it had been so easy.

I wanted to be brave again.

I wanted to realize a dream that was actually my own and didn't involve applying a mask compiled of thick makeup before stepping on stage into an inauthentic role I'd forced myself to play. I'd started to realize that what got me to a certain level of "success"[14]—the Monkey had gotten me noticed—was now holding me back.

I wanted to put the lessons and life coaching I'd been learning into practice, but since I rarely left my apartment and was in the process of shedding people from my life, I'd have to try those lessons out with people I'd never met to see how the new shoe fit. To see if in fact Rhonda was wrong and that I could turn my ship around, let go of the anger, and calm the Monkey.

So I packed a bag and left.

Now let's be clear, this was not an epic *Eat, Pray, Love* journey for many reasons. Chiefly, I had a little dog to worry about and a shrink to see, so an epic six- to eighteen-month journey was out of the question. Instead, I would go, often alone, or in small groups of people I'd never met before, on a two- to three-week trip while an ex-boyfriend or a neighbor watched Karl. While there was pray-ing involved,[15] I never had a problem with eating, and frankly, love was out of the question. I resolved to stop dating for a while[16] and deal with my trust issues. I also wanted to give myself some time to figure out who I was and what I liked, and to chill the heck out before looking for a mate—because past experiences had shown me,

---

14. I use air quotes around success as, looking back, I never felt success-ful. Even though I was making a ton of money for a few years, was featured in all sorts of glossy magazines, was feted at parties by all sorts of rich and famous people, I still, deep down, felt like a fraud.

15. Which mainly involved sentiments like, "God, please get me out of this alive," or "God, can you please make these antibiotics kick in now?"

16. A "while" turned into years. Yes, you heard me right—YEARS! Sometimes things take a little longer than you had planned.

if I was an angry mess who didn't know what she was looking for beyond the superficial, I would end up attracting an angry, superficial man. I also wanted to take sex out of the equation, relearn how to be friends with single, heterosexual men, and step out of my comfort zone of gay men.

But, like *Eat, Pray, Love*, it was a journey of self-discovery.

In a way, traveling in a small group or alone is the most effective way to put new life lessons into practice.

The journey was rough going at first. While Rhonda calmed down, the Monkey went into overdrive doing parlor tricks for entertainment. During one early trip to Kenya, I acted as a sort of fortune-teller, bragging that from my years as a gossip columnist, I'd become a "social anthropologist"—a bullshit, arrogant term whose meaning I wasn't even sure of. I'd boast I could see a train wreck coming a mile away, blahblahblah, and then tell people, "I can tell if you're an only child, the youngest, or the oldest, or if your parents are divorced, or whatever" after just five minutes of meeting them.

While some of my guesses were right—at least on a superficial level—many of them were wrong.

I look back on my assumptions, judgments, and the armchair shrinking—which was so arrogant and just blatantly awful—and I cringe. I think I cringed while I was doing it, which is why, after the last trip to Kenya, I stopped.

Somewhere along the line, after I'd allowed myself to get to know someone and be pleasantly surprised yet again that they weren't who I thought they were, I started to realize that maybe all my judgments and "rules"[17] were wrong.

---

17. With the exception of "life is about timing and lighting—and you can only control one." I will never disavow that one! Do not try to get me to sit down at a restaurant that doesn't know the power of a dimmer . . . and I probably would not go on a second date with a man who is rude to the waiter on the first. Unless there were serious

I used to proclaim these rules all the time. Things like "never trust someone who doesn't have friends of their own gender," or "men over a certain age (which would fluctuate depending on how old I was getting) who have never been married are damaged—watch out!" Now I think: *Well, maybe they were smart enough not to get married too young to the wrong person. Maybe they hadn't found the right person yet and weren't willing to settle. Maybe they needed to figure some shit out about themselves first before they committed to someone. Maybe . . . they were just like me.*

Which is weird for me to admit. I was raised in a house of women. My father wasn't around for much of my childhood—and when he was, I'd wished he wasn't. The result was that for much of my life, men, in general, were either authority figures to be impressed or sex objects . . . the female version of the Madonna/whore complex many men have.

That is not to say that sometimes people's actions don't seem familiar to me. But now, instead of saying THIS IS WHAT YOU'RE DOING AND WHO YOU ARE! I will internally note the red flag, shut up, and keep moving. Because maybe that person is just having a bad year. I now try to reserve my judgment and give people the break I have so often needed.

It was during my trip to Mali that I learned how to get along with vastly differing personalities for an extended period of time—some of whom I didn't particularly care for and whose personalities, to me, were like nails on a chalkboard. Part of getting along and maintaining peace is to not always have to voice your opinions, feelings, or thoughts, because, sometimes, speaking your mind (or at least the thought of the moment) can create more damage. On a boat down the river Niger with six others, one woman (we'll call her Jenny) had frayed my last nerve. I said something snippy, a

extenuating circumstances like the waiter was his second cousin who once slept with his mother or something like that.

precursor to a larger takedown, and the rest of the group, en masse, turned and shut me down in two hot seconds with a collective hiss. At first I was taken aback and annoyed, but I quickly realized what the others already knew. If I had gone one sentence further, it would have messed up the rest of the trip for everyone. It would have been a divisive play for a moment's respite. A day later, I challenged myself to an experiment in which I played the game "What Do I Have in Common with Jenny? I Bet I Can Find Something Loveable about Her." Turns out, we had a few things in common. And I quite liked Jenny by the end. We even e-mail once in a while.

I learned in Mali and Brazil that to be divisive or cohesive is a choice. There is always a moment when you can give in to jealousy and baser instincts or you can celebrate others' achievements and differences.

In Vietnam I found the truth that anger, intolerance, and ignorance lead to death. To fight and die for an acre of land or to protect someone else's ego is futile and senseless.

In Iraq[18] I discovered that, even without the Monkey, I am great company and that I am a loving, caring person willing to protect and nurture others at my own expense. I learned about true undying love from Marie, a Belgian woman. Marie had lost her great love, an Iraqi diplomat who'd been assassinated a year earlier, and joined the bus tour because it was the only way for her to visit his grave and say good-bye (Iraq didn't allow single tourist visas below Kurdistan). Then there was the bravery of Niall, the eighty-year-old

---

18. Yes, I "vacationed" in Iraq. During the war. It was for a piece I did for *Playboy*, in which I got on a tourist bus (the only one) and traveled all over the country looking at ancient Biblical sites from the Old Testament. As fascinating as the sites were, even more so were the people on board—a mix of adventure junkies, elderly people who wanted to see the sites, and a few tomb raiders.

Irish man, who had, several years earlier, walked across Afghanistan[19] and wanted to visit the historic religious sites of Eden, Ur, and the birthplace of Abraham to pray for his dying wife.

There was the cruise to Europe, in which I learned that with proper boundaries (no talk of religion or politics), my dad and I could not only get along but also discover a real friendship despite past hurts. When things did look like they were going to go weird, I sat back, took a deep breath, and reminded myself not to take things personally. Because they weren't personal. At all. It was just Daddy being Daddy—and I needed to accept him as he was, not as I thought he should be.

Along the way, there were some people who didn't understand why I traveled so much. A TV producer friend once looked at me and said, "Are you ready to stop running away now?" and I knew he didn't get it. Because I wasn't running away from anything—I was running toward something . . . running headlong into situations in which I could not only try out new lessons in coping and dealing, but through which I could also forge a new path for myself that didn't involve the comfortable grooves and ruts of my old life.

He didn't understand that sometimes to gain perspective, you have to physically remove yourself from the situation and find silence.

Part IV: New Growth

Now comes the part in the story where the frog turns into the princess . . . sort of. Because the trek for me is not over. It will never be over. I still travel as much as I can, and more importantly, I am still learning new lessons and ways to look at life. I wish I could say there was a checklist I could offer—something where I could look at

---

19. Saying, hilariously, "Of course I walked across Afghanistan! And did it by myself—who's gonna bother me? I'm eighty. I'm no threat to anybody."

people and say, "Compassion? Oh yeah—draw a line through that. I got that one *down!*" or "Rhonda? That bitch is long gone!" But she's not. She's still grumpily rambling around my psyche. I slip and stumble and sometimes feel like a Paula Abdul song ("I take two steps forward, I take two steps back . . ."), but I now know there is a time and place for both Rhonda and the Monkey. Rhonda, if left to her own devices, will ruin my self-esteem. But she is actually a good warning system. After all, without her, I might have done a raging wildfire burn, and left my job with no savings and no plan, instead of a controlled burn. And the Monkey? Well, let's be honest. A well-fed, tame, happy monkey is fun as hell. And still great company at a dinner party. Or on a cruise.

There are a few truths I have come to know. As Buckaroo Banzai said, "Wherever you go, there you are." You can try to outrun your issues—you can get another job, change apartments, move cities, travel, or go out every night of the week. But you will still be you. Whether or not you are hiding in your closet, traveling on a ten-hour flight, driving in your car, or unpacking the boxes in your new house, the blaring fact is *you* will still be *you.* Geography changes nothing. If you don't sit down and meet your own Rhonda, she will hound you until the end.

I have also tried to ease up on my judgments, if only because I've had to. I look back and laugh—not in a "Ha-ha, that's hilarious" way, but in an "Ooh, karma got your ass" Schadenfreude kind of way—when I realize everything I ever said I'd never do and sometimes blatantly mocked, I have now done. This is gonna get embarrassing. For example:

- Be an unmarried woman of a certain age with no kids who, instead, has a little dog she anthropomorphizes to such an extent that he has his own personality, his own Twitter handle, and a full-on winter wardrobe? Check.

- Mess around with a married man? Check.[20]
- Get so desperate wondering what the hell I'm doing with my life that I visit two psychics, an astrologer, and a voodoo priestess? Check.
- Cheat on a boyfriend I love? Check.
- Own several self-help books and not only read them but *take notes*? Check.
- Do "hippie" stuff like meditate every day and attempt to do yoga? Check. Semi Check.[21]
- Shun bacon, butter, steak, and anything else that was ever on my Top Ten List of All-Time Yummy Foods in favor of raw-food shakes that include things like flaxseeds and spinach, because I have cholesterol levels that are through the roof? Check.
- Set my DVR to *Oprah's Lifeclass*? Check.
- Go to a plastic surgeon for Botox, Restylane, and something called a "vampire facelift"? Check.
- Walk around in my pajamas and not shower for *five days straight*? Check.
- Create a loving, healthy relationship with my mother and father? Check. Thank God.

Along with the aforementioned realizations come a lot of apologies.[22] Learning how and when to apologize is humbling and empowering.

20. In my defense, I thought he was separated.
21. I am not that flexible.
22. And by apologies, I mean taking accountability. I am not talking frivolous bullshit apologies—or the ones that people with low self-esteem issue for, you know, everything including their very existence. I am talking "Oh man, I really messed up and didn't mean to. This is my fault" apologies. Things I have found myself apologizing for in the past four years: thoughtlessness, rudeness, lateness, cursing,

We are all human, we all make mistakes—hopefully ones that aren't fatal or don't cause deep, hard-to-mend fissures—and at some point, we must all apologize. Sometimes just to ourselves. For being so harsh on ourselves, for not seeing our own fabulousness or beauty, or for physically beating ourselves up in the form of crappy diets, sexual promiscuity, or forcing our fragile egos into toxic company.

On that last point, I am now very conscious of who I spend time with. It is very important to surround yourself with people who not only think the best of you but also hold you to a higher standard and inspire you. Someone's energy will affect you, and you will mirror it. If you have to be around a miserable pile of poo because, say, you are stuck on a two-week trip with them, learn how to separate and maintain a mental distance.

These days I try very hard to be honest while being kind with others, but especially with myself.

For me, one of the most important lessons was learning to shut up. That whole reality-star movement of "I Have to Talk Constantly Because I Tell It Like It Is" is bullshit. Most people are just trying to get attention, and what they think of as "telling it like it is," is really just some judgmental baloney their Monkey is screaming. Half of the things that you think should be said should not be. In fact, people will appreciate you way more if you just listen. Because, after all, every one of us just wants to be heard, and the most precious gift you can give someone is your full attention. If they ask for your opinion, and only if they ask, you can give it. The void doesn't always have to be filled and should be respected.

---

writing items on people during the gossip column days and really hurting them in the process, forgetting birthdays/engagements/anniversaries, forgetting the names of people whom I have known for years because I never bothered to learn them in the first place. You know, those embarrassing, awful apologies.

Some time after I'd quit my job, I ran into a woman named Daisy at a party for my friend Tom Sykes's book.[23] Daisy and I were having a fun little conversation as we both smoked cigarettes[24] outside the party, when out of the blue she stunned me. I present that part of the conversation in its entirety:

Daisy: You're so nice.

Me: Oh, well, thank you—I try!

Daisy: You know, we've met before.

Me: We have? I'm so sorry. I don't remember.[25] Please know it's nothing personal . . .

Daisy: It was at polo on Governors Island.

Me: Yeah, I remember the event—it was like a month before I quit my job—so I don't think I remember much else. Was I hideous?

---

23. Not everyone I know has written a book—I swear! But the ones who have, have written amazing ones. Try Tom's tome—*Blow By Blow: The Story of Isabella Blow*—available online! You'll love it, I swear.

24. Yes, I know. It's an awful, disgusting habit, which according to my mother will cause me "to have an unusually disgusting painful death." I am in the process of quitting. One vice at a time, people, one vice at a time!

25. Now, back in the day, when confronted with something like that— as I was all the time—I'd lie and say, "riiiiiight, yes, of course!" and then fake it through because I didn't want to hurt anyone's feelings—or more importantly, I didn't want to look bad. If someone is not remembered, it says they're not important, right? It makes me look like a total blockhead . . . or worse, someone who doesn't pay attention to people unless they are "important." Ugh! I hate those people! I didn't want to admit I could possibly be one of those people, but part of my trying to release the Monkey was trying out this whole honesty thing. And to be frank, I had spent The Angry Years in a fugue.

Daisy: No, not at all. You were very funny. But you just seemed so . . . angry.

Me: Fair enough . . .

Daisy: I don't mean to sound awful, but you just seem so different right now. You're still funny, but you're just not angry any-more—and you're very nice.

Me: Thank you. I'm trying.

When I recounted this story to others, they would gasp and say, "How awful!" But I never felt that way. In fact, it had the opposite effect on me. I was quite proud and happy to have tangible outside acknowledgment that all my efforts were not for naught.

This past fall I interviewed Suze Orman for the Sundance Channel as part of a web series I created to promote the channel's show, *Dream School*. During that interview, Suze said something that stuck with me. A light clicked on when she said: "I do not think I am successful just because I have money. I'm successful because I love who I am, and I have no regrets. And I'm successful because I have a great heart and I have compassion and I care and I would be happy with or without money. Now with that said, lack of money sure can make you miserable, but I don't think I'm suc-cessful because I have money. I think I'm successful because I know who I am."

And then, right there in that studio, I knew I was finally reach-ing a meaningful level of success.

I'm successful because I know who I am.

Mine is not the standard, tangible story of "success," as in, I hit rock bottom and now I'm a shiny, rich, super STAHHHH. I don't have a high-profile job. I'm still a freelance writer working on another book. I have run through most of my savings and still live in a small rent-stabilized apartment in New York. I can't remember the last time I went dress shopping or traipsed down a red carpet.

But that's okay—because those things aren't in my standards of success anymore. I am a star, at least in my own life. I also know I haven't reached my full potential. Don't get me wrong, I'm still Paula Froelich. As in, I AM PAULA FROELICH. But I'm not quite (and please say this in an Oprah Winfrey voice) PAULAAAAAA (motherfucking) FROOOOOOOOELICH! Yet.

I'm still learning who she is.

6.

IT IS NEVER TOO LATE TO CHANGE EVERYTHING

Leslie Bradshaw

Courage is not the absence of fear, but the triumph over it."
—Nelson Mandela

D espite the popularity of the Obama "Hope" poster from 2008, the fact remains: hope by itself is just wishful thinking.

But with courage and deliberate action, hope can actually become real change. Whether you are an entrepreneur looking to responsibly leave the company you helped build, or living in a situation that is negatively impacting your well-being, or just in need of some change in your life, I promise you that my story has something instructive and inspiring in it for you.

Starting at the age of twenty-four, I helped turn a talented designer's web-design and branding "side business" into a full-fledged creative agency.

And not just any creative agency. We were *the first* creative agency to visualize Twitter conversations for the 2008 presidential election with C-SPAN and Tropicana, respectively. We were *the* creative agency that pioneered the use of infographics as a consumer-facing marketing tactic (starting with the first version of the Conversation Prism with Brian Solis in 2008). We were *the* creative agency that led the first geo-social check-in from space with NASA and Foursquare. We were one of the smallest agencies to do some of the biggest data-driven storytelling projects with Samsung, Nike, Intel, American Express, Twitter, Facebook, and Google—and we did so *directly* and not under a larger agency like most folks our size. We increased our revenues by thousands of percentage points from 2006 to 2012 and, as a result, were named to the Inc. 500 list not once, but twice.

The year I turned thirty (2012), we were named "Small Agency of the Year" in the southeast region by *Ad Age* and my talented designer partner and I were named to *Inc.* magazine's "30 Under 30" list.

And not just any talented designer. In the earliest days, Jesse was my boyfriend first, my business partner second. In the final days, he was my business partner first and my boyfriend second.

Leaving was hard. Really freaking hard. Jesse and JESS3 were all I had known for six years. Leaving meant I was leaving my business partner *and* my boyfriend. It meant saying good-bye to clients with whom I had done groundbreaking work. It meant bidding farewell to coworkers with whom I forged bonds on par with the strongest steel thanks to our time in the hot furnaces of project hell.

Make no mistake: My departure was something that I carefully weighed, expertly planned, and seamlessly executed. It took equal parts acceptance, confidentiality, coordination, confidence, resoluteness, and courage. It also required two sage guides who had done it before (David and Karen, mentor superheroes you'll learn about more later)—as well as countless friends and family members—to help me see the forest through the trees.

Why leave something you built and someone you loved? Because they darned near killed me. It sounds hyperbolic to say, but stress and depression are real things that can rob you of life (even if you still technically have a pulse). Running a virtual, "multinational" company exhausted me and stressed me out. The differing approaches that my former partner and I had was as upsetting as it was depressing: he was the creative genius and lone wolf, I was the pragmatic businesswoman who grew up playing team sports. Never the two shall meet. The Sisyphean task of trying to make every single stakeholder happy—from clients to team members to Jesse—was so frustrating that I felt defeated and deflated more often than not.

All told, it took me four years to recognize, accept, and finally take decisive action. This wasn't a linear journey and it wasn't without moments of bargaining with myself. But ultimately, I summoned the courage to take my wishful thinking and turn it into real change.

This is the story of where the beginning of the end all began, how and why my health and happiness started to suffer, and the not-so-linear steps I took to acknowledge that I needed to make systemic changes, face my fear of change, and develop and execute a deliberate action plan to enact the change. Buckle up; it's about to get real.

Dancing Backward in Heels and Holding Two Double-Edged Swords

Starting a creative agency at twenty-four years old with a partner who is also twenty-four years old means you have the distinct *advantage* of being more digitally native than your competitors, but the distinct *disadvantage* of not knowing how to run a company.

Want to make it even more complicated? Date your same-aged cofounder (we were born exactly four days apart, both bull-headed Tauruses at that). Much like the digital-native double-edged sword, dating the guy you are building a company with brings both good and bad things. The "good" thing is that your every waking moment is focused on the business. We brainstormed in bed, we counted work sessions as dates, and even tacked on vacations to talks we gave in places like Spain and New York City and conferences we attended in places like Miami, Vegas, and London (and by "vacation" I mean working from a different and often very nice location). As efficient as it was, the "bad" thing was there was very little actual space for any sense of an "us" outside of the "we" of the company.

So there I was, dancing backward and in heels carrying two swords that had blades on both ends. As many women and entrepreneurs had done before me, my team and I were doing the "Ginger Rogers" to keep up with "Fred Astaire." That is, we were doing everything the big agencies were doing—producing work, winning clients, and managing our business—while also dancing backwards in our heels. Our metaphoric heels here represent the fact that we were struggling to look graceful and like we had our shit together all while building infrastructure, managing across time zones to leverage the best talent, undercutting the "Fred Astaire" prices from the big guys, and learning the hard way that youthfulness does not an expert make (even for digital natives).

I was also doing this complicated dance on a personal level. I was my boyfriend's chief operating officer and his girlfriend. I couldn't show weakness in either role, lest I fall behind his aggressive "Fred Astaire" pace. In addition, his e-mails and directives to me could be read only one way (with far more expletives and all caps, might I add): Dance Ginger, DANCE. Faster Ginger, FASTER. Better Ginger, BETTER. I loved the challenge in the beginning, but even the greyhound eventually gets tired of chasing the electric rabbit. But I am getting ahead of myself . . .

Building Your Ship While Sailing on Someone Else's

So where were we? Ah yes, the early years. For the first few years of building the company, I was still working at a series of full-time, nine-to-five jobs. Each taught me critical things I applied to the company I cofounded, including (but not limited to) how to run the financial side of a business, how to (and how *not* to) manage and motivate people, how to see a project through from beginning to end, how to position yourself in the marketplace, how to develop your offering, how to service clients, how to write reports and memoranda, and much more!

OK, saying my day jobs fully "taught" me and I truly "mastered" each aforementioned skill might be a stretch in some cases. Saying my full-time jobs "gave me insight into" might be a more accurate characterization when it came to the larger infrastructure and project processes.

Either way, it was exhilarating, exhausting, and instructive all at once. In order to build this company and still deliver results and advance in my day job, I had to work over fourteen hours a day for three and a half years (2006–2009). I crammed as much as I could into each day and into my tool belt. I was living dog days; each day felt like one human week. I felt like a superhero in disguise, running circles around my peers while the circles grew around my eyes.

However, as much as I wanted to believe and will it otherwise, there just wasn't enough time to learn it all, to perfect it all, to apply it all.

The not-so-secret secret was this: I was making it up as I went along. Sure, I had so-called learnings from other jobs. And of course, there was what I "learned" from so-called experts at industry conferences in London, Miami, New York, San Francisco, and other hyped-about locales. Oh and don't forget about all of 'dem "learnings" that I gleaned from reading countless blog posts and books by other entrepreneurs who had come before me.

But let's get real: no amount of all-nighters, workshops, on-the-job learnings, reading, listening, good intentions, or even acting it out on someone else's dime prepared me for running a company. I had to go through the pain of making mistakes and learning the hard way.

What a paradox those early days were! So much confusion and exhaustion that I would give anything to not relive them, and yet there were also many professional breakthroughs and enlivening experiences that I wouldn't trade for the world. The early days brought me to dozens of cities all over the country and all over the world. I drank in the cultures and people and technologies I encountered. Each of those experiences opened my eyes wider and wider to my professional potential. I somehow managed to take these trips and still run the company with only a few hitches. I credit Google Docs, Basecamp, Skype, an amazing team, sugar-free Red Bull, amazing schedulers, my mostly indefatigable body, and my totally unbreakable spirit.

For the first time since my nerdy academic days in school, I felt like I had a powerful purpose and the means within myself to actualize it.

Together with my team, I broke molds, won awards, and had Fortune 500 brands knocking down the door of the company I helped build. The future was boundless.

"A supposedly fun thing I'll never do again."—David Foster Wallace

In January 2010, I finally left my full-time, nine-to-five job and doubled down on the on-the-brink-of-greatness company I had been building during my nights and weekends for the past four years with Jesse. I resigned as the director of engagement from the agency that helped me grow as an account, project, campaign, resource, and people manager. Oddly enough, I found it hard to say good-bye to the very stability and infrastructure that I sometimes fought. How does the saying go? You only miss it once it's gone? Works for corporate structure as well as relationships, it seems.

Up to that point, I had thought I was working hard when I had two jobs. Boy was I wrong. When I decided to focus entirely on what we were trying to build, I found out that I had a whole other reserve of energy from which to draw. I can only liken my state to what I hear from my friends who have children—they say that you somehow get this surge of energy, hormones, and survival skills that propel you through the insurmountable tasks at home and at work, all while running on very little sleep. While I didn't technically (er, *biologically*) give birth to offspring, I had helped give birth to a company, and as it grew, just like a child, I was looking out for its well-being.

Each day would start with my heart pounding before my eyes even opened. My to-do list was never ending and my mind liked to run through it whenever I was trying to rest. Morning. Night. It didn't matter.

Another thing that was always on? Jesse. He would always be up before me working on his computer, and would look back at me when I started to wake. No loving morning greeting. Nope. Just a quick-fire series of questions: "Any good e-mails? Any good tweets?" My already heightened heart rate managed to jump a few more beats. Ba-boom! Ba-boom! Ba-boom! It rang in my ears.

Monitoring our brand, new business pipeline, and project docket started around eight a.m. A quick check-in with our team in England over IM, sometimes Skype, was next. They were all senior directors and were humming along in a midafternoon work trance. On a good day, we would leave them alone and let them chew through their similarly infinite task list. On a less good day, we would request about forty-seven new things before they logged off. It was common for our creative director, Christian Day, to stay up until four a.m. his time to support the team to the finish line. "I think my eyes are bleeding," he would chat at me. I hoped they weren't, but understood the severity of his metaphor and fear they might actually be bleeding.

Then the walls of back-to-back conference calls started. I know what you are thinking: *Boohoo, Leslie. All of us have our productivity killed by conference calls.* I hear you. But have you ever taken one on your computer while being *simultaneously* dialed into a second one? While you are e-mailing and IM'ing to give directions and answers? And (mostly) pull it *all* off? I bring this up not to brag (OK, maybe a little to brag), but rather to illustrate that literally every minute of my time was double, triple, and even quadruple-booked.

The only appointments I broke were with friends, family, and myself. If I remembered to eat before five p.m., it was a good day. If I didn't, then around nine p.m. hunger pangs would overtake me and we (Jesse and I) would place an order at one of northern Virginia's many eateries. We ordered nearly everything on whatever menu we had in hand (Domino's, P.F. Chang's, Chef Geoff's, Maggiano's, The Liberty Tavern, The Italian Store, the list goes on). The bill would often soar north of a hundred dollars, and when the food arrived (or when we schlepped it home after ordering takeout), we would feast like soldiers back from a victorious battle. Silverware optional.

When the team in England logged off, and the cross-country team members all had what they needed (from Brooklyn to Oklahoma City to Orlando to Los Angeles), and the clients quieted down (usually by ten p.m.), I could finally get to my bigger-picture work. Writing POV white papers, memos, and decks. Drafting custom strategies for RFP responses. Reviewing our pipeline, pro forma, and invoice system. If I had a lot to do, I wouldn't go to sleep. If I got inspired, I wouldn't go to sleep. If I was nervous about dropping something at some point, I wouldn't go to sleep. The only time I actually slept is when my body literally gave out. And even then, I could squeeze out a few extra hours past, say, three a.m. if I had "Sweet Disposition" by The Temper Trap on repeat and Red Bull. In fact, I played "Sweet Disposition" over seven hundred times between 2010 and 2011 (Thanks, iTunes, for keeping track of that stat!). And when we finally got an office, Red Bull gave us a free fridge for our loyalty and patronage.

The pressure was immense: we had six-figure contracts with Fortune 100 brands. The stakes were high: we were responsible for the technology behind live events on which clients had eight figures riding. I reveled in the challenge of it all.

One might argue that resoluteness and loyalty ran even deeper in my blood than my astrological sign (Remember? I am a bull-headed Taurus). My ancestors came across the Oregon Trail six generations ago and homesteaded in Idaho and Oregon. I am convinced that thanks to their pioneering spirit and determination that led to a successful journey and to bountiful lives as farmers, I have embedded in my DNA the ability to persevere and prevail in the face of great challenges. To my Baskett (two *t*'s) ancestors from my mom's side: thank you and may my resoluteness honor your journey!

These traits further manifested themselves in my belief that I could make a positive impact on anything I did . . . if I just worked hard enough. If I just cared enough. If I just loved enough. If I just bounced back enough. If I just sacrificed enough. If I was just patient enough.

"Leslie, you are a fool if you think you are going to make this work," they all said. To my face. Behind my back. There were a lot of reasons they said this to me and behind me. They didn't think I could date my cofounder and run a company with him. They thought his personality was too difficult to partner with in either arena. They didn't think we could win contracts with elite brands like Nike and Google. What's the saying? Haters gonna hate? Yes, that's the one.

Their doubt and disbelief fueled my passion and perseverance to, in fact, make. it. work. "I will show them," I would mumble under my breath and through clenched teeth. "I will turn their 'haterade' into water and then walk on it. And then I will turn that into wine and drink it," I would say to myself as I watched the sunrise, feet tingling from not having moved in hours (perhaps days).

I remember seeing a bright burst of light outside at around six a.m. one fall morning that year. I hadn't been to sleep in over forty-six hours thanks to one of the hurricanes that was a perfect storm of client demand, team-member demand, boyfriend–business partner demand, and long-form writing and thinking demand. This magnificent light came as sort of a beautiful shock to my eyes, so I took a photo and posted it on Twitter. A prominent DC publication then linked to me and said of my pre-Instagram Twitpic: "local technology company president Leslie Bradshaw greets the morning." Little did they know I hadn't been to sleep for over forty-six hours, and the rising and falling of the sun meant very little to me, other than to signal some sort of passing of time that told everyone else it was time to go to bed or to wake up.

By the end of 2010, we had taken our revenues from the tens of thousands into the millions. Our client roster lit up with the hottest household names. I was exhausted, and I could see my team was, too. And yet I was strangely fulfilled and alive. All at once.

My Lifeline Read: ABORT! ABORT! ABORT!
In February 2011, we moved out of our respective home "b'offices" (what the team and I affectionately called working from bed) and into our first physical office (aka the "p'office"). With a central gathering place and a reason to put pants on in the morning, I had renewed hope that we would retain the zany creativity that had become our calling card, but that we would forgo the chaos that was wearing all of us down. That's what growing up was all about, right?

This hopeful feeling would last exactly one week.

Before we could even unpack our boxes or order unique office kitsch from Etsy, I invited one of my mentors, David Reimer, to sit with each of our team members one-on-one to assess where we were as a company from their points of view. He delivered his assessment back to me and to do so, borrowed a line from Dickens: "What you have here Leslie is the best of times and the worst of times." Adding context, he went on to say, "The projects are exciting, the clients are prestigious, and the team would go to the end of the earth for one another. But there is physical fatigue and emotional exhaustion that runs deep. I see it on your face and on theirs."

Well then, there you have it folks. I wonder if this is how Sisyphus would have felt if he had a mentor pull him aside to explain that what he was doing was going to have no productive end.

What followed David's assessment was the first "get real" talk that I was ready to hear about the state of my professional (and by extension, my personal) life. The operative phrase here is *ready to hear*. Over the course of the years between 2006 and 2010, my friends, family, and colleagues had all been trying to deliver variations on the message David delivered to me.

The difference between this time and those previous red flags was that I was finally ready to listen because the chaos, lack of sleep, and stress were wearing on me. He had my attention. So when David relayed his insights from the last thirty years of watching companies grow, succeed, and fail, a rush of sobriety ran over me. With every hair on my body standing on end, I was alert like my life depended on it. Given how much of my identity and relationships were bound up in the company, my life *did* depend on it.

I could help win and execute tons of amazing business, but nothing would matter if it came at the cost of my well-being (and the well-being of others). I was essentially pushing a rock up a hill, only to have it slide back down again and again. Yes, I made huge gains in terms of revenue (the up part). But barreling back down the hill at me were my failing friendships, strained time with my family, my once exuberant love of life, my on-edge-all-the-time attitude, and my no-longer-healthy body. My skin, weight, hair, smile. They were all suffering not-so-silently in front of the mirror and the world.

One month after taking in David's advice, I went on a two-day retreat to a peaceful coastal town in Maryland with one of David's colleagues, Karen Vander Linde, who specialized in operations and in succession plans. The goal of the weekend was to look at the two possible paths I could take. On the one hand, how could I improve the current situation by making changes in process, protocol, and personnel? And on the other hand, what would it look like for me to do something different altogether—and do so in the most professional and responsible way possible?

Karen and I rode bikes around the beach town. We turned off our phones. We shut off our computers. We went analog. The February ocean air was salty and crisp. And inside of me, the fog lifted from my brain long enough to make sense of a few critical things. Rosy cheeked, we came back inside from our bike ride and sketched our lifelines on white paper with deliciously smelly markers (strawberry! licorice! watermelon! lemon! orange!). The lifeline exercise is something you can do at any point in your life. To get started, draw a horizontal line in the middle of a large piece of paper and mark it 0. Above the line is +10, and the lowest point below it is -10. Look at the 0 line as your x-axis, and label the beginning point, on the left, "age zero" and the end of the line on the right "current age." For me at the time, I was plotting data for my twenty-eight years of life.

At Karen's instruction, I mapped out the most memorable highs and lows in my life. I marked high points such as succeeding in school academically and athletically, falling in love for the first time at fifteen, and getting engaged at eighteen (reader take note: these affections were for two different guys, Ryan and Eric, respectively), and winning my first six-figure and first seven-figure deals in my twenties.

The low points captured a move from Lake Tahoe to Oregon in middle school, broken hearts from good and bad boys alike, and the moment I currently occupied. As I connected the dots in order, an erratic heart monitor line—like an electrocardiogram—appeared in front of me.

But even more than the ups and downs (which are to be expected in life), I was shaken by just how low I had marked my current state. Lower than my most brokenhearted moment. Lower than my at-the-time life-altering move away from my friends when I was in the sixth grade. This simple exercise and visualization had me realizing just how bad my current state was. It was bad. Like, *really* bad. The worst moment in my twenty-eight years of being alive. Shit.

What made it bad? The exhaustion. The lack of joy. The differences in management and relationship styles between Jesse and me. And the interplay between the three. They managed to amplify the dark corners of one another, allowing them to synergistically join forces and darken my once bright lighthouse. Even the things that would have brought me +10 joy when I was younger became burdens in this dark state.

Take for instance the moment I was named one of *Fast Company*'s five "Most Influential Female Tech Executives" in 2011 (alongside four heavy-hitting all-stars: Marissa Mayer, Cher Wang, Carolyn Leighton, and Mary Meeker). Instead of congratulating me, the first thing out of Jesse's mouth was, "That's a lot to live up to. I hope you are up to it." Ya think? Of course, that was an intense and accomplished group to be with, but then I took a beat and reflected to myself, *They are each beyond impressive, but did any*

of those women found a company at twenty-four? Without taking ven-
ture funding? And generate $13 million during her tenure? No, they
ran other people's companies or founded something later in life. I
had earned the accolade and planned to not only live up to it, but
pay it forward by mentoring other women and continue to strive
for higher heights (as an aside, I landed on *not* another top *women*
Fast Company list two years later, but the hallowed "Most Creative
People in Business" list for "making data science cool." What's that
line from Sarah Lacy—once you're lucky, twice you're good? Yep,
that's the one).

Now to be clear, the problem wasn't that I didn't like working
hard. It actually was that I liked it far too much. And it wasn't that
I couldn't handle the ups and downs of working with my significant
other. It actually was that I was far too committed and loyal to the
idea of it working out to see the simple fact that it wasn't ever going
to work out.

And if I am being completely honest, I was also scared of what
the alternative looked like. Like, watching-a-scary-movie-with-
chainsaws level of fear. What would the industry say? What would
the clients say? What would the haters say? What would the fox say?
It wouldn't be until 2013 that I would get definitive answers to all of
these questions. Spoiler: the answers to these questions were far better and at the same time far worse than I could have ever imagined.

Coming out of my retreat with Karen, and with help from my
former "number two," JESS3's third employee, and close friend
Becca Colbaugh, I took my first four steps to creating positive
change in my life.

First, I set real goals, deadlines, and step-by-step, detailed
actions. My goal was to be happier and, deep down, I knew that
that would mean leaving the company I built and the guy with
whom I built it. I knew it would take a long time to responsibly

throttle my role down with clients, large projects, the team, and the finances, so I gave myself until the end of 2012. I also didn't let myself get away with just goal setting; I needed to "step set." To start living a happier and healthier life, I fully understood the first step was acceptance and the last step would be leaving JESS3. But what was really overwhelming—and frankly paralyzing—were all the steps in between. How was I going to detangle financially? How would I communicate with clients? What would my next venture be? These were all questions I spent months answering, mapping out, and preparing for.

Second, I got serious about implementing advice from sage advisors. There was always a steady stream of people giving my partner and me advice over the years, but because we were running and gunning all the time it was hard to stop, reflect, and integrate their wisdom. From this sprung new processes, new roles, and new protocols. As with any sort of change, these were met with some resistance, but overall people appreciated the upgrades and the good intentions. In particular, more standardized work hours and templatized proposals meant that some of our once boundless creativity was, well, becoming bound.

Third, I started planning the company's move to Los Angeles. Not only was there a higher density of potential hires in LA that fit the kind of roles we wanted to fill, but two of the company's most experienced and senior leaders lived in LA. If we were going to seriously scale, have more balance, and continue to do groundbreaking work, we had to be in a place like LA. I set the date for early 2012 and began working on what was going to be needed from the team and from me between now and then.

On a personal level, I needed a break from Washington, DC. I needed to go somewhere that had fewer reminders of the best and worst moments of my life. After moving there in 2005 to be with my former fiancé (Eric) and immediately beginning a relationship and a company with Jesse, I was ready for a change of scenery and pace.

Fourth, I stepped on the scale. This was something I hadn't done in years and frankly was terrified to do. Although weight is not an end-all-be-all metric in life, it is a surefire way to determine if you are living a healthy and balanced life. Well, the results were in: I had gained fifty pounds since starting JESS3. This was devastating to a woman who had competed athletically in some variation of skiing, dancing, softball, volleyball, basketball, and weight lifting from age two through the age of twenty-four (the age that, not so coincidentally, corresponds with the moment I started building JESS3, *ahem*). But like the lifeline exercise with Karen, the number on the scale and the reflection in the mirror were simple visualizations that helped me realize that things could only get better from here. This was my physical rock bottom.

I spent the remainder of 2011 implementing our new SOPs (standard operating procedures) and hitting the gym at least four times a week. I also cycled through the 17 Day Diet Plan a few times. Sticking to a diet and exercise routine while trying to manage the chaos that came with running JESS3 wasn't easy. In all honesty, the "new me" didn't actually stick until I stepped back in a big way upon arriving in Los Angeles. As long as I was the last one on the line, taking panicked client and employee calls at all hours of the night, and putting everyone before myself, my weight loss would be superficial at best and fleeting at worst. I dropped about twelve pounds, and by the time I was boarding the plane to Jackson Hole, Wyoming, to be with my family over the holidays, I finally felt like things were actually getting better.

But this feeling would last exactly three months and one week. I gained a lot of the weight back leading up to, during, and after a trip to Austin, Texas. Let me explain . . .

The Temporarily Calming Effect of Queso and Teamwork

The annual technology industry's "prom" is the thing that reminded me that I was Sisyphus in need of a *Shawshank* escape, despite my Joan of Arc and Spartan tendencies. Like many in the technology industry, I have a love-hate relationship with South by Southwest (SXSW). We all love it because it brings together so many friends and movers and shakers in one place (and a cool, funky, weird one at that). We also love it for the keynotes and the occasionally stellar panel, provided you can get a spot in line early enough to enjoy them. But when it comes to the reasons I particularly hated it that year, mine were not quality-of-content, unbearably-long-line, lodging challenges, or hangover related. No, they were entirely connected to the stress, anxiety, uncertainty, urgency, and immediacy of having to manage, curate, and visualize data on gigantic screens for paying clients.

When I landed in Austin on the eve of the SXSW Interactive Festival, it was raining and unseasonably cold for mid-March in Texas. My team was already boots on the ground, setting up for our client (a large tech brand hired us to visualize social data on enormous monitors in the main convention center), so I stood alone at the baggage carousel until it stopped moving. Despite being on time for my flight, the airline had managed to lose my oversized, zebra-striped suitcase on a direct flight from Baltimore. Yes, I said direct. And yes, my luggage was unforgettably zebra-striped. A customer service team member assured me that they would "send it to my hotel when it came in." OK. That worked. Next, I needed to get a cab. Once outside, I saw what appeared to be a cab line that was wrapping back around itself. If I didn't know any better,

I would say it looked like people were lining up to see the Jay-Z/
American Express concert or the Seth MacFarlane keynote (both
highly anticipated events slated for later in the week).

I took a deep breath and got into line. No bag, rain splattering
at my feet. It was in this moment that I muttered to myself, "Could
this day get any worse?" And of course, when you say things like
this, it is as if you are tempting the universe to answer your snarky
attitude with an emphatic YES.

That's when the text messages started hitting my phone. To say
my phone was "blowing up" would be an understatement. I was
ready for the thing to have smoke billowing out of it, the text messages were coming in so fast. My heart rate quickened with every
buzz. Nothing was going right on site, and I was hearing it from
every direction (let your imagination take those "Ginger, dance
FASTER! BETTER!" statements above and make them as bad as
you can imagine . . . and then multiply them by a thousand).

In that bag-less, cab-line-for-days, text-message-fireball moment,
two things became so clear to me that I nearly jogged the whole way
to the Austin Convention Center.

First, there was nothing I could do to calm the barrage of text
messages . . . except maybe go get some Tex-Mex for the team. While
I couldn't get involved in the behind-schedule project directly, I
could bring the team Torchy's Tacos. And guacamole. And queso.
And chips. And caffeinated sugar drinks. And give them smiles and
support. As soon as I got into my cab, I had the directions pulled
up, and the driver and I rushed over to 311 South First Street as
fast we could within the law. One hundred and fifty dollars later,
I was loading what felt like a few hundred pounds of beans, meat,
tortillas, chips, macerated avocados, melted cheese, salsa, and sugar
water into my patiently waiting cab.

I also ate my weight in said provisions on the ride over, derailing
my diet and helping pack back on a record five pounds in a week.

Stress didn't just make me want to eat, it also made my body want to hold on to the extra pounds. There is some interplay between serotonin and cortisol that I will never understand fully but enough to know that the lack of one and the prevalence of the other has always spelled weight gain for me.

Second, this would be my last SXSW under these conditions. Like a valiant bull rider, I held on for my eight-second ride once. And then twice. And there was nothing left to prove. Not to mix metaphors here, but I was ready for my jersey to be hung from the rafters.

After delivering the tacos to the team and scarfing down some myself, I doused as many "fireballs" that were flying at my team as possible, and then headed to my hotel only to find out that—wait for it . . . wait for it . . . they gave my room away. Remember how I wondered if things could get any worse? Well, consider the hotel room being given away my rock bottom moment.

Let There Be Light, Life, and Love

Then the rain broke. And they found me a room. And my luggage arrived. And my cousin, who lives in Austin with his wife, texted to let me know that they had just given birth to a son. I hopped in a cab, and I went and stayed with them for what felt like hours. The experience was so life affirming. And family affirming. And relationship affirming. To meet my little cousin Luke. And to see his parents love each other and love him with every ounce of their being.

Waiting at the hospital for a ride back to the convention, I had another burst of clarity and came to a third conclusion right then and there: I was done living the way I was living. It was the most euphoric feeling in the world to see what true, unconditional love looked like thanks to my cousin Larry and his wife Kirsten (and to know what it *didn't* look like thanks to the dark place I was living in with my boyfriend–business partner).

I needed to tell someone about my epiphany. I couldn't yet tell my team. And it was much too late to call my parents by that point. Luckily, two of my longtime friends and mentors just so happened to be at SXSW. I grabbed a late dinner with Dave Gryce (my first boss in DC and professional idol) and then met up a few hours later with Joe Chernov (coconspirator and life inspiration are the best descriptors for him). With tears in my eyes, I explained my decision. And with tears in theirs, they told me that they couldn't be happier for me. Not because I was leaving something I loved, but because I was leaving something that was clearly hindering my health and happiness.

I promised Joe and Dave and myself that when I got home, I would not only follow through with my plan to move the company to Los Angeles but would also finally make the choice and plans to leave altogether. Being the deadline-driven operations executive that I was, I gave myself a deadline of the end of the year.

Picking Up the Pieces So I Could Start Packing Them Up

Back from SXSW, I faced the reality of the promises and deadlines I made for myself. I also faced the aftermath of the fireballs that had been hurled at our team from every direction at SXSW. My turtle shell wasn't strong enough to protect them, and as soon as they found something else, nearly 100 percent of the people who had worked on that project resigned. It was a déjà vu moment, since we had gone through nearly the same sequence of events the year prior.

What was driving away these talented, creative, and hardworking soldiers at the same time every year? Was it some weird migratory thing? Alignment of the planets? No, that's far too complicated a read on the situation. It was pretty simple why they were leaving. They were working on too many projects at once. They were having to execute projects whose scope creep turned a straightforward project into a "make it do this and this and this and also this while still being able to do this" project. And to exacerbate their pain further, like me, they weren't sleeping very much and were receiving similar "EXPLETIVE! GINGER" e-mails and IMs from every direction.

How did we get there in the first place? Too many reasons to list, but let me try. The desire to make the client happy got us there. Saying yes to too many requests and no to, well, none. Overselling the capacity of the agency *while also sending most of the team to Austin*, expecting that somehow they would have "down time" to work on other client projects. Having deadlines slip on other projects leading up to March further exacerbated this "perfect storm," as did having a perfectionist CEO who wanted to be hands-on when it came to every detail of every project. I loved Jesse's commitment to excellence; it was a vision we shared in life and in founding the company together. But I did not love that he wasn't flexible when the situation warranted it; time, budget, other projects needing attention meant that throttling down to 80 percent was sometimes a must.

As I decompressed from SXSW 2012, the old adage came to mind: You know what doing the same thing over and over again and expecting different results is? The commonly accepted definition of insanity. I also realized you can't please everyone all the time, so don't try.

It was also *super* hard not to tell anyone about my plan. This was in part because I didn't want to leave anyone in a tough spot professionally and financially; my company employed parents, newlyweds, and folks who were recently engaged. This was also in part because I had lived so many lives with each and every team member, fighting in battle after battle alongside one another. This, my final battle, was to be the hardest and yet loneliest of all. But I am glad I remained stoic; the older I get, the more I realize you don't have to tell everyone everything. It gives you more options and doesn't burden people with the heaviness of your truths.

How do you not tip your hand? You keep working. And when you can, you give others the chance to "step up into a new role" by offloading your workload. In retrospect, I am sure my team would read the signs differently. But at the time, most everyone took my move to LA as a sign that things were heading in the right direction and the fact that I was "pulling back" as a healthy, long-overdue move they were happy to see me making.

My Final Step to Freedom Was Just Three Suitcases and Six Months Away

On my thirtieth birthday, I started packing up my 464-square-foot apartment in Georgetown. And instead of shipping my seventeen boxes to Los Angeles, I shipped them home to Oregon. I packed only three suitcases to live out of until the end of the year. Just enough clothes to wrap a few large projects, get through the 2012 election, and responsibly depart the company I helped build from the ground up.

The team in DC would dwindle to just a few and the p'office paraphernalia (a good forty-plus boxes' worth) would be packed up and shipped to the east side of LA. I posted pictures to my social networks of the move and bid Washington, DC, a big thank you and a fond farewell. No one looked at the shipping labels and just assumed I was all-in for my move to Los Angeles. But I was one foot in, one foot out. I secured a short-term lease on an apartment in Pasadena, California, and rented my furniture. I was a modern gypsy.

For the first time in years, I felt alive again with equal parts purpose and hope and freedom that I knew wasn't passing. The feelings were the roots that had shot off of the hollowed-out trunk of my old self. With enough water, sunshine, joy, execution-against-my-master-plan, patience, courage, and exercise, I knew they would grow strong in the months to come.

I worked out with a trainer twice a day for five months. I slept ten hours a night. I ate five small, healthy, protein-packed meals a day. I bought a membership at a spa and got a massage on a monthly, sometimes even weekly, basis. I got my nails done once a week. I started interviewing at various companies and putting my feelers out carefully and quietly: *Leslie Bradshaw was on her toes and on the market.*

At first, it felt like I was being disloyal to the company I built and the guy with whom I built it. Heck, we were still boyfriend and girlfriend (and we would be up until I resigned in late November 2012). But I quickly reminded myself that leaving was already in motion, and once I left, I needed to have a job to show that I wasn't a victim of agency or boyfriend burnout (because I wasn't!). It was less about making money, I had plenty saved up. As much as I wanted to curl up in a ball and live on my family's farm in Oregon for a while (forever even), Joe Chernov's words reminded me that I needed to not look defeated. And I needed to obey the law of inertia and stay in motion.

A few months into executing my plan in LA, a friend and mentor based out of Miami, Freddie Laker, called me up to share the project he was working on. It was so futuristic and backed by such smart money, and he was such an incredible person with a depth of experience that I craved learning from, that I called him the next day to ask for a job. I flat out said, "I will be the best number two you will ever have."

I had a new job to look forward to and a boss-partner that would bring me to the next level professionally, without sucking my light and soul in the process. And in the background of my rediscovered love of sleep, eating right, working less, indulging more, and exercising, I lost another seventeen pounds.

The final days were nigh. Which brings me back to the burning question: How do you leave something you built from the ground up? That grew up with you as you grew as a professional? That was made from the blood, sweat, tears, bubble gum, chicken wire, energy drinks, queso, and passion you and a handful of well-intentioned people piled together? I will tell you what: It is darn near impossible to leave, because you don't just derive your income from this thing you've built. No, you in fact extricate your very sense of being and purpose.

But I finally realized and accepted that it wasn't just *the* path forward, it was the *only* path forward.

That Which Nourished Me Almost Killed Me

As you've come to learn from my story, the company I helped build, my former boyfriend–business partner, our team . . . they were all my greatest joy. Combined, they were also my single most exhausting endeavor. They were what I woke up thinking about, and they were the last things on my mind as I collapsed onto my pillow at night (provided I was even going to bed that night). They were my everything.

But on November 27, 2012, leaving it all is exactly what I did. On that fateful Tuesday, I walked away from something I had taken from being a graphic designer's side business to a full-blown company that cleared over $13 million in revenue over the course of my tenure as president and chief operating officer. After six wonderful, trying, joyful, hard, enlightening, and exhausting years, I handed in my resignation to Jesse, thanked him for everything, high-fived him for all that we accomplished together, and wrapped up the conversation by breaking up with him. Walking out of the most private of the offices in our LA studio on the east side of LA, I then began telling the staff one by one, as quickly as I could. My team was expert at viral marketing, after all, and I wanted each and every staff member to hear it from me if not first, at least in earnest.

"Get busy living, or get busy dying."—Andy Dufresne (Played by Tim Robbins in *Shawshank Redemption*)

Following my communications with Jesse and the rest of the JESS3 team, I posted an announcement on my Tumblr blog, thanking everyone and offering a teaser about my new job without naming it just yet. I sent out over four hundred e-mails to friends and colleagues—and called as many folks as I could, too. I updated my LinkedIn, Facebook, Twitter, SlideShare, and another half dozen online profiles. I stuck to the script that I had written myself all summer. It was the greatest and most important campaign I had ever strategized and executed (even more important than the first geo-social check-in from space!). The only thing I didn't plan for was the response—it was pure love, gratitude, and support. I sat in my empty Pasadena apartment out of breath, tears pouring down my cheeks. My mom there to comfort me and keep our packing schedule on target. Aren't moms just the best?

I did it. I survived. And when it was time, I let go. And not a single fear came true. I realized that I had lived far too long in denial and fear and that my mind was what kept me prisoner far more than anything or anyone.

I took the entire month of December off. My in-box was completely silent for the first time since 1997 (back when I signed up for Hotmail and no one had my address yet). I ran out of things from my old life to talk about, so I just started commenting on the weather and the height of our creek (locally pronounced "crick") with my parents. I went on ten-mile walks. I put away my phone and just looked out over endless fields of emerald green and listened intently to everything anyone said to me. I heard clearly. I saw clearly. I went to bed at eight p.m. I was there for my mom, dad, sister, and nonagenarian grandma like I had never been.

I moved to Miami on December 28, 2012. And that's when the life I was always meant to live started to really unfold.

I landed an apartment on the twenty-ninth floor of a building that gifted me a two-hundred-degree view of Biscayne Bay, downtown Miami, and South Beach in the distance. The sun hits the water every morning and taps me on the shoulder to wake me up. I do some yoga and then head down to my gym on the seventh floor, where my trainer Deemsy Arias is there to work me over like a borrowed mule. I've lost another twenty-five pounds working out with him and even more importantly, gained the strength to lift, and pull, and push just about any amount of weight. After my workout, I head back upstairs, eat my freshly delivered paleo meal from Clean Food Co in Miami, hit the shower, and take an elevator down twenty-four floors to my office to start my workday. All by ten a.m.

My new team and I built a software product that turns text into video, so for the first time in my recent professional memory, I have the luxury of time, reflection, listening to consumers, and the ability to iterate on my side. We also have the benefit of a physical office (p'office!) and of all being in one location from the get-go (gone are the eye-bleeding, "multinational" days). Our CEO, Freddie, works as hard as he does smart. He has loyalty from team members, clients, and former colleagues that I could only have dreamed of having in a partner. He calls me boss, and I call him boss-boss. And while I may in fact be living up to being his best number two, he is my best number one.

I went from never having enough time, to having too much of it. I've realized that you can never be your best self without extra bandwidth to think clearly, give to others, and appreciate sunrises and sunsets.

Thus, with this gift of time and mental bandwidth, I decided to mentor about a dozen people who had reached out to me, advise a handful of companies (some for equity, some just for fun), write more, read more, sleep more, work out more, and date for the first time since I was seventeen. At last count, I have written and verbally delivered over a hundred references for all the professional "soldiers" with whom I fought from 2006 to 2012. There has been no greater sense of joy and accomplishment than to help others. Especially for those who sacrificed so much of themselves at my behest.

As for dating . . . it took going on a few average and a few above average dates for a good six-month period before I found someone really, really special. Special enough for me to want to open up and share on levels I hadn't let anyone access since I was engaged to Eric back in 2001. While I am uncertain where things may go (which is hard for someone as type A as I am), I do manage to pause often and give thanks for *feeling* and *caring* deeply about someone like this again. What's more, the gentleness and respect I receive from this new guy has helped heal my heart. As hard as it has been over the last ten months to not have all the answers, the gradual pace has helped me keep perspective and to stay true to the pledge I made to myself when I left JESS3: my health, my family, and my friendships would never be sacrificed in the face of a company or a guy ever again. Our budding relationship has also reminded me that I love to . . . be goofy, build pillow forts, make out in cars like a teenager, laugh at my own jokes (usually as I am telling them), read/share/discuss/learn about random and interesting things with someone, and get all dolled up for a guy that's as worthy as he is worth it.

Through this relationship, I've realized many things, but perhaps the most important is this: to find and be with a better man, *you first have to work on yourself and become a better woman.*

Saving the best for last, I want to take a moment to talk about the evolution in my relationship with my family. My mom, dad, and sister have always, always, always been there for me, and I am freaking thrilled to finally give them the very best in return. Mary Ellen Bradshaw, Jim Bradshaw, and Jennifer Bradshaw: I am sorry I didn't heed your advice earlier, and I am infinitely grateful for your unconditional love and support through thick and thin (literally and figuratively). When things got so overwhelming that I just wanted the lights to turn off and never come back on, you were the shining lights that kept me going. Skyping, WhatsApping, texting, and Facebooking like we do now throughout the day makes me so happy. And even though many miles separate us (as we are spread across Oregon, Dubai, and Miami), I love that we are prioritizing trips to visit and have adventures together.

Laugh often. Know love. Be healthy. Find true balance between work and life. Count your blessings on your fingers and toes. Give the best of yourself to those who are most deserving. Let your grace unfold. Smile out loud. I know all of these feelings and states of being once again. And I wish that you may know them all, too. For it is in fact never, ever, ever too late to change everything.

7.
WILLING TO BE LUCKY

Glynnis MacNicol

I have never had a résumé.

This is not by design—I don't have anything against résumés—it's just that I've never needed one. I don't note this as a point of pride, either, but simply because, as much as anything, it seems to neatly sum up how I've approached my career, which has, at almost all times, been less the result of planning than of timing and a willingness to say yes.

I find myself leaning on this small truth of my professional life when I'm approached by people of all ages who are looking for guidance as they navigate the tricky waters of employment in this new digital age. I'm especially aware of it now that I find myself in the position, as the cofounder of a group aimed at elevating professional women, to be doling out advice to young female graduates eager to map out their own paths and looking for guidance about how they might do so.

It's where I often stumble. Because when you are someone who started out with no plan of your own—and no regret about not having had one, by the way—it can be tough to advise others on how they might learn from your successes. (But what about *your* mistakes, you say? Too familiar and prosaic to bother you with.)

What am I supposed to tell them? Trust your instincts? See what happens? Leap without looking too hard? Do as I did? I moved to New York on a whim, landed a job waiting tables at a still-legendary bar (more on that shortly), and through timing and hard work navigated my way rather quickly up the ladder of both book publishing and media. This sort of counsel, though it may be true, feels both irresponsible and not a little insulting. People, including me, like maps and signposts and some reassurance that they are headed in the right direction. And, as the essayist Kurt Andersen once wrote, the flip side of leaving yourself open to chance is that you must also be willing to be unlucky, and that's scary. This is not exactly the sort of life plan one can easily take home to Mom and Dad following an expensive college education.

And yet, especially in this new professional world, which we all occupy to some degree—where new industries seem to be popping up and then disappearing at a dizzying rate, where two years is considered a long time to spend at any one company, and people with strange job titles that often include the words "social engagement" can (currently anyway) make a sizable living—there is perhaps some reassurance to be drawn from the fact you can still get from point A to point B without actually knowing the route when you start out.

In fact, I would argue my ability to stay open to opportunity regardless of how it arrived, and jump on it regardless of whether or not I could clearly see the outcome, is the exact thing that enabled me to not only survive but thrive in the often terrifying upheaval that plagued so many professional worlds (in my case, the media industry, which in many ways has felt like ground zero of the digital shakedown) in the last ten years, and do so when many far more experienced and accomplished folk sank amid the turmoil.

"No one should come to New York to live unless [they are] willing to be lucky." E. B. White wrote this in his famous *Here Is New York* "love poem" to the city, and I've often thought of it when I've considered my career arc, which happens to have transpired entirely in New York. The word "willing" suggests that luck is as much a lifestyle choice as any other path we set ourselves on, and just as much or as little under our control.

I don't know if it's more common these days for women to come shooting out of college with clear and ambitious career plans in hand, as though it were a mathematical equation they've been working on since childhood, than it was when I was finishing high school in the midnineties. But it certainly feels that way. My sense now is that so many of the young women I meet who are just starting out have been considering their career path for nearly as long as they've been able to spell the word "career." Recently, while researching an article about the higher levels of burnout among the so-called millennial set for a national women's magazine, I spoke to a series of twentysomething women who all seemed to view their twenties as some sort of Olympic-level event. One that begins with landing the exactly correct job straight out of college and that will (hopefully) culminate somewhere around age thirty with an executive-level position and a marriage followed by two children before the now-magical fertility age of thirty-five that we are continually threatened with by a media intent on ringing our biological alarms.

I have to imagine some of this has to do with the Internet. "You can't be what you can't see" is a phrase I hear with increasing frequency these days, and use myself, generally in relation to women and minorities attempting to find their way in professions long dominated by white men. However, the same sentiment seems oftentimes to have been reworked in this era of social media into "You *should* be everything you are seeing." And Lord knows, there is so much to see.

To the best of my recollection, this was not the case when I was finishing school, and for that, I am mostly grateful. Sure there were the handful of ambitious folk who liked to toss out phrases like "Rhodes Scholar" and "medical school," but despite the fact that many of the women I've known since high school lead very successful professional lives, I have no memory of any real discussions with friends about what we were planning on doing with our lives, or how we'd do it, or even the sense that high school was simply the opening gambit in a larger game in which everyone was merely setting different game plans in motion. Obviously, there was no social media then, beyond the gossip passed around over the Christmas holidays at actual gatherings with friends, so it's entirely possible I was simply unaware of the minutiae of other people's ambitions, but the sense was that we had plenty of time to figure things out.

I certainly had no career plan other than to jump as far and as fast into what I perceived to be the deep end of life and immerse myself there. If pressed, I may have admitted some vague ambition involving writing, but mostly I think I was simply excited to be on the move. The world seemed like a very big place and I was eager to experience as much of it as I could. To me, experience didn't just trump ambition, it was the soul of ambition. It was the only thing that mattered.

Part of this mentality I think is simply timing. As in, the result of the time I was born in—namely the seventies—which was not that long ago but can sometimes feel like another age entirely. Particularly when you consider that when I was in university, it was still the norm to send handwritten letters home; wait for the film to be developed in order to see whether you were in fact snapped at the right angle; and lose touch with people you went to high school with. In the last few years, I've gotten in the habit of telling people I moved to New York before the Internet. That when I first arrived here in the late nineties, I was immediately advised by those in the know to linger in front of the *Village Voice* offices on Astor Place every Tuesday night and wait for the rumbling newspaper trucks to deliver that week's issue, so I could get to the back-page apartment listings before they hit the newsstands and subsequently make a run to the nearest pay phone. (It would be a few years before those same in-the-know people would begin whispering the word "craigslist.")

In other words, not that long ago—let's call it before Facebook, so really less than a decade. We knew a little less, and moved a little slower, and life (or at least your ability to meet up with friends on any given night with the precision of a heat-seeking missile) was left slightly more to chance. So perhaps it's not entirely surprising that when I started out, I was more willing to let the chips fall where they may than I might have been had I come along ten years later. I sometimes wonder if luck may be weirdly harder to come by these days when so much of the world is discoverable without actually moving, when gut instinct often feels as though it's been replaced by SEO results, or Klout score ratings, or Facebook profiles, or Instagram accounts. Not that I don't enjoy these things also, or that I pine for the days before Seamless (I don't), it's just that I think it may be more difficult to rely on timing and opportunity as a way to get by when nearly every new lifestyle development is geared toward scheduling our lives in an increasingly streamlined fashion. We know so much all the time and we have come to depend so heavily on that access to knowledge, if not our own then the group's, that we don't spend any great time not knowing. These days, not knowing actually requires a determined effort. And yet there is so much power and opportunity to be had in the not knowing.

That's what I did and what I still try to do to a certain extent, and perhaps just being aware that it's possible to not plan and to still be OK may be an antidote to the endlessly agonizing career guidance and "how to network" posts I come across with such frequency. Along the way, I've picked up a few lessons that I still hold near and dear.

Always say yes. Almost everyone has a waiter or waitressing story to tell, or they should. When your income depends entirely on tips (I don't know what the rules are now, but when I was doing it, the base pay for servers was something like two dollars per hour), you very quickly learn to become an expert in human nature. Either that, or you go hungry.

It is common knowledge among those who have held server jobs in New York that there is a lot of money to be made in restaurants. (That Lena Dunham's character in *Girls* remains a barista instead of angling for a job on the floor of a restaurant, where she might have made four times the money in one-fifth the time, has always been some signifier to me that Dunham's New York City street savvy suffers some blind spots.)

I had a couple of server jobs early on, but the restaurant I worked in the longest was an old-school New York bar located in the heart of Greenwich Village, famous in its time for being frequented by abstract expressionist painters like Jackson Pollock, beat poets, and later Bob Dylan. During my stint, it was a locus for neighborhood locals who treated it as a second home: NYU students; artists; musicians; a few business types; remnants of what remained of the blue-collar population below Fourteenth Street, once the mainstay of the city; and movie stars who liked to be treated like normal people. Some customers, including one Oscar-winning actor, had been coming in for so long they'd have their mail delivered to the bar when they were out of town, or call in their Super Bowl picks from far-off film locations. Some had individual drink prices. It was the sort of place that still honored the three-drink buy-back, but where the customer was never right—a fact widely acknowledged by the surfeit of regulars and often a surprising discovery for the less familiar crowds that tended to swarm in on a Saturday night.

Tom Wolfe once described it as the *cénacle des cénacles*—forever translated to me by those in the know as the "circle that connects all the circles." And while Wolfe was referring to the painters who congregated there in the fifties, it always seemed like an apt description to me of what it was like to be in a place where it frequently felt like the whole world, with its endless opportunities, was being showcased nightly in the form of paying customers. The staff turnover was so low that getting scheduled permanently on a Wednesday- or Thursday-night shift—coveted because the customers were all regulars, low maintenance, reliable tippers, and went home by midnight—was the server equivalent of landing a rent-controlled apartment with high ceilings. And almost as rare. People did not leave this job any more than the regulars changed their nightly drink order.

It was arguably the best server job to be had in the city, the kind you might find in movies or novels but rarely come across in real life, the sort of experience that provides both a lifetime of lessons and an endless supply of the sort of stories we tell ourselves in order to live. And the reason I landed it is that I overheard someone at a café in SoHo talking about how much money a person could make there.

"He who hesitates is poor," goes the saying, and at that moment, still in my first year in New York, I happened to be very poor. It was the middle of summer, the worst time to get a service job in a city that emptied out in July and August, and I'd recently been fired from a short-lived gig in a Nolita bistro, where I poured glasses of wine and prepped salads, after the owner discovered I was a Virgo and felt this was incompatible with her Aries. "It cannot possibly work," I recall her saying as she handed me my hourly wage in cash and saw me to the door. I remember very clearly that I had exactly fifty dollars to my name, in cash (one thing you learn from being truly broke is that money is relative—that fifty dollars felt like an absolute fortune to me as it was the only thing between me and . . . I wasn't sure, but I learned how to make it stretch in an effort to keep whatever it was as far away as possible). I was subsisting on a large bag of lentils I had bought for two dollars at the corner bodega and cooked a cup at a time in the pot I'd purchased at a dollar store when I'd first moved in. I had ten days to come up with rent.

In my heart, I suspected the man I'd overheard had been exaggerating. The staggering amount of money he'd mentioned seemed so far-fetched to me at the time that part of me assumed he'd been telling a story, not relaying a fact. But I went anyway, immediately walking the fifteen blocks and grateful I was wearing black so the sweat stains I was incurring from the raging July heat wouldn't be too apparent when I arrived.

I think if I hadn't been so desperate, I might have been more nervous. The place, an old tavern with wood-paneled walls and rows of back booths, appeared completely empty when I arrived, and the door banged as I came in, like a cannon announcing my arrival. It was cool inside, an immediate relief from the blazing sidewalks, but also very dark even though it was high noon. It took me a few minutes to make out the soaring, intricately carved bar that lined one wall and then, slowly, the bartender behind it. I felt like I'd been called onto a stage alone to account for myself to an audience I couldn't see. But I stood my ground, asked to see the manager, declared I was looking for a job, and, when asked, assured them that absolutely I had waited tables before (I hadn't, but at that point, it was figure it out or go hungry, and I concluded it was better to get my foot in the door than not—this remains true to this day). I agreed to come back the next morning to train. On the way home, I bought myself a two-dollar egg sandwich at the Sidewalk Café on Avenue A.

I don't remember what I learned during that Saturday morning training session, just that I spent the day in a state of extreme anxiety, suffering that feeling of deep ineptitude that a new job almost always brings on. But I had showed up, and when, at five p.m., one of the staff called in sick thirty minutes before the Saturday-night shift, I offered to fill in.

That night is a blur. (In fact, it ended up being eleven hours of such nonstop chaos that even after all these years, I am still prone to nightmares about it.) Actually, it felt like going to war, if war were conducted in a small restaurant in the middle of New York City that served five-dollar martinis and deep-fried bacon atop hamburgers. What I remember most clearly is that I spent the entire time running—from the customers to the bar to get drinks, from the bar to the kitchen window to get food, from the table to the service station to find water glasses, to clear ashtrays, to place orders, to clear dishes. And then back again. And then again. There was no busboy to help and no break until the bar closed at four a.m. I wrote everything down everyone ordered, most of which didn't make sense to me and then sounded out drink names at the top of my lungs to the bartenders, always requesting the drink "neat" when I'd forgotten, or didn't know to ask, whether the customer wanted ice (easy enough to deliver it on the side if need be). When I was wrong, I learned quickly to apologize to the bartenders, who wielded all power (benevolently, it must be said, as many of them are still close friends), and discovered the power of the word "sure" when it came to customers (Them, accusingly: "I ordered that with ice." Me, calmly: "Sure."). I learned not to sweat the details (Was there garlic in the chicken marsala? I had no idea and no time to run the twenty feet to find someone who could tell me. Better to say yes like I meant it and have them order something else than take the time to find out).

But mostly I learned to learn on the run, and also to know that I could do so, a talent that served me well many years later when I leapt into the blog world. I also learned to pay attention, which is something that has served me in every job I've held since. People will show you who they are, Maya Angelou once said, and this may never be more true than in a restaurant, partly because food and drink are such basic human motivators and partly because, as I said before, when you work for tips, you become extra attuned to signals that let you know what sort of tip you can expect. In the restaurant, this meant that more often than not I could tell what sort of customer a person would be before they were ten feet past the door: the way they banged open the door, the way they made eye contact, what drink they ordered (Jameson on the rocks meant 20 percent, Stoli with Coke meant 15 percent tops). In my later careers, it has often meant knowing when (and when not) to ask certain questions of interview subjects, or employers, or employees. Or how to gauge from a distance the intentions of people who are approaching me. Or even how best to enter a room while picking up on the small gestures that can tell you so much about the other people entering it: what they might want or be afraid of letting you know they want.

The next morning, four hours after I'd returned home reeking of cigarette smoke, having spent seventeen hours on my feet, I came back for my second training session. And then, when the same server remained out that night, I stayed on again to work the Sunday-evening shift. By the time I finally got back home at three the next morning, covered in dried mayonnaise, with revoltingly swollen ankles, I'd made my rent for the next two months, landed a regular schedule, including the Saturday-night shift, and found a way to not just stay in New York but live there.

All you need is ignorance and confidence, and the success is sure. Practically speaking, beyond paying my rent and providing me with a number of lifelong friends, that job not only opened my eyes to all variations of what life could look like in New York City, but also grounded those lifestyle choices in real people. In a very real way I was able to see how all the other halves lived and that helped me recognize, at least in my own mind, the gap between where I was, working for (albeit terrific) tips, and where I might want to be (and, for that matter, where I definitely didn't!).

When the mother of one of the young women I had hired to work as a waitress, knowing I harbored vague ambitions of writing, asked if I wanted a job in book publishing, where she herself was a top agent, I saw that door to the next phase open itself a crack, and once again, I jumped through. I knew exactly nothing about the publishing industry except that it was where books were made and that I liked to read. Nevertheless, on my friend's mother's recommendation, and following a quick interview in which I talked about my reading habits, I found myself out of the server world and into the realm of the foreign-rights scout (for a great deal less money, I should note).

This time, instead of drink orders and hungry customers, I was navigating my way through the deep end of book publishing: meeting with established editors and agents, creating relationships, and finding sought-after manuscripts before anyone else saw them in order to advise the foreign publishers I represented (much of the money in publishing is generated through foreign sales) on whether they should bid on them. It was heady stuff. Again, I found myself being forced to learn on the run and to say yes to things with a now-growing confidence that I would figure it out as I went. Publishing is a notoriously slow industry; editors start as assistants, working their way up the professional ladder for a long time before reaching a position with any sort of power. Scouting, on the other hand, is a cutthroat niche within the business that requires one to be always on the run and juggling every aspect of the industry at once.

Consequently, within a year, and after taking every meeting I possibly could, I was being sent to the international Frankfurt Book Fair and meeting directly with the heads of publishing houses.

However, the more time I spent reading other people's writing, and helping make sure it reached publishers, the more I wanted to be writing myself. Perhaps nothing is more clarifying career-wise than seeing up close someone else do what you want to do.

"Hola, chica, do you chat?" One morning, a year or so into my publishing career and still in the early days of Gchat—before I even quite knew what the green dots along the side of my Gmail screen meant—a window popped up in my e-mail screen. A number of years earlier I'd taken a Mediabistro writing class along with a lawyer named Rachel Sklar, and we'd stayed in intermittent touch. She'd gone on to launch the media page at the newly created *Huffington Post*, which at that time was only two pages in its entirety, and was looking for contributors. Seeing my green dot online in the early hours every morning, Rachel reached out to ask whether I wanted to write something.

I had never blogged before, which I think at that time put me in the majority. Blogging was then considered, and remained for some time, something people who couldn't get real writing jobs did. To get a "real" writing job, a person often began by doing small pieces, event listings or restaurant reviews in magazines such as *Time Out*. Then you would take your "clips" and mail them (literally, in the mail) to an editor with a pitch.

I did not have a real writing job, but I knew I wanted to write. Two months later, in February of 2007, when Rachel was looking for someone to take over the morning news roundup for her *Huffington Post* media blog, *Eat the Press*, and she asked me if I'd be interested, I simply said yes and quickly penned a post about Andrew Sullivan moving to the *Atlantic* (a post that remained my top search result for many years) to prove I could string sentences together. My media knowledge at the time was fairly limited to what I'd read on *Page Six* in the *New York Post*, arguably the most powerful page in newspapers at the time along with the *New York Times* op-ed section (cf. Paula Froelich's "Controlled Burn" essay in this collection), and seen on *Charlie Rose*. I'd never heard of Keith Kelly, then the most widely known media reporter in the city. I think it's entirely possible I didn't know who *Gawker* founder Nick Denton was. And my understanding of how the nuts and bolts of blog posts actually worked when it came to HTML was pretty much nil. But I did know I wanted into this world very badly and that the door, or in this case the Gchat window, had been opened a crack.

Here's how it worked. I would get up at five every morning, scan the Internet for news, go for a run around Prospect Park, come back and do my news roundup, leave it in draft for Rachel to look over, get on the train (spending the entire time terrified I had spelled a name wrong or missed a story), and be at my desk by nine thirty a.m.

Sometimes I would arrive in the office to e-mails from people who didn't like how they'd been described; from time to time, I'd arrive to an e-mail from Arianna herself. In the evenings, after a full day of scouting work, I'd be out at either book parties or media parties that Rachel would take me to (where I quickly learned you should never write something about someone that you can't defend to their face, because if you are remotely good at what you do, you will soon find yourself in that situation) and get home sometime after midnight. Then I'd get up and do the same. For four months.

When the presidential debates started that spring, my workload doubled. Twice a week, on average, Rachel and I and a guest writer would live-blog each debate (Twitter had yet to take hold, and live-blogging was still new and useful—we would paste our comments into a Gchat window, and Rachel would then transition them to the *HuffPo* WordPress system). On those nights, it wasn't unusual for me to arrive home after two a.m. But it paid off. By that June, I had hundreds of bylines and was getting paid to write for the web, which still felt like a guerilla operation and not yet the mainstream wrecking ball it would become a year or two later.

Being in book publishing, however, as it felt the early crunch of the rise of e-books, was an awful lot like sailing on the *Titanic* (it would be another year or so before the digital iceberg would decimate newsprint). So the next spring—after more than a year of filing news roundups and blog posts, attending media galas, and paying my own way to the New Hampshire primary, where Rachel and I ended up in the spin room with every major political reporter in the country following the famous "You're likeable enough, Hillary" debate—when a spot opened up at the Mediabistro blog *FishbowlNY,* I took my *HuffPo* bylines, a big leap (and a significant pay cut), and jumped on board the Internet full-time. For the next year, I would be paid twelve dollars per post to publish a minimum of eight posts a day on the subject of the New York media industry.

Admittedly, this move seems smart in hindsight (even if I did spend that April crying in my accountant's office). Sailing onto the web in 2008, especially on the media/politics beat, was one of those decisions greatly helped by timing, in my case, the combined timing of the digital world and the election of Barack Obama, which by then was driving an inordinate amount of news coverage. In the moment, however, more than a few people whom I held in great respect thought I'd lost my mind for leaving a promising job in the book industry for the untested, likely temporary, waters of the blogosphere. The consensus was that I was leaving a foundering ship for a soon-to-be-sinking raft. But I knew I wanted to write and that the door would not stay open forever, and by then I'd become accustomed to taking risks and making leaps, so I ran through this next door as fast as I could.

Career-wise things got a bit easier after that. *FBNY* happened to be one of the few places online covering the media industry, which was still thriving (in an "and the band played on" manner) with nightly parties attended by veteran luminaries (I lived on hors d'oeuvre trays out of financial necessity that year), and as a result, I spent most of 2008 immersed in a powerful media world that would, unbeknownst to us at the time, more or less cease to exist a year later. Furthermore, it would become clear that I'd actually landed myself a front row seat on a seminal roller coaster. In the summer of 2008, after cold-pitching the editor in chief of *Playboy* on the idea that the magazine should be running an election blog, particularly considering how Hillary's candidacy was electrifying parts of the country, I was sent by the magazine (and paid a magazine salary, to boot) to cover both of the presidential election party conventions (if there is a greater opener than "Hello, I'm here covering this for *Playboy*," I have yet to discover it).

Alas, it was not to last. By that fall, along with the financial markets, much of the magazine and newspaper world collapsed. I quickly went from the early stages of a traditional magazine career to spending every Friday afternoon waiting by my computer for the inevitable news dump revealing which magazine had folded or which staff had been laid off. After I'd posted the news, as often as not, I'd spend the evening attending a consolation drinks get-together with the newly unemployed. My low-paying risky perch at *FishbowlNY* suddenly seemed like one of the safer gigs in town. And as I watched so many people with careers I had deeply envied not long before flailing about in a new digital world that required a nimbleness and risk-seeking usually native to the young (it's no coincidence that the last five years have seen the rise of the twentysomething CEO), I became increasingly grateful for and increasingly dependent on my willingness to take leaps and learn as I was running.

been to pay my own way to somewhere I want to be and something I want to do. I got my first real newspaper byline in May 2000 on the front page of the sports section at the *National Post* in Canada. Was I lucky the editor accepted my pitch, or was he lucky that I'd paid my own way to Saint Petersburg, Russia, to run around the World Hockey Championships for two weeks with no press credential other than a notepad, a tape recorder, and hope?

There was no luck involved in filing a piece on the World Cup of Lawyers from Malta, other than knowing that there was something called the World Cup of Lawyers and that it was being played in Malta. Okay, there was some luck involved—with 45 teams of athletic, highly educated men from 21 countries, the ratio of men to women was nearly 20 to 1. I don't know what was in the water in Malta, but my hair has never looked worse. It didn't matter. Malta was fun. (Plus, luck is in the eye of the beholder. I was unlucky to step off a curb and break my foot at the Republican National Convention in 2012, but I was also lucky that I didn't break two feet.)

It's good to acknowledge your own privilege, and I do. I recognize how lucky I was to grow up in a lovely Toronto suburb in a terrific, supportive family with a decent genetic cocktail, including being white in a neighborhood that was exclusively white and going into a profession—all my professions, actually—where the defaults favored (and still favor) people who are white. I recognize my own autonomy—not everyone can hop a plane or even a BoltBus at a moment's notice.

But consider this example: You appeal to your employer to attend a great industry event. Your very reasonable request is politely declined. "We'd love to send you to X conference, but we've already got Y and Z going!" you are told. "We simply don't have the budget for any more!" And off Y and Z will go to said conference, leaving a trail of party photos in their wake while you sit in your cubicle and stew.

I hate stewing. I'd much rather do things that feel important and exciting and expanding and edifying and illuminating, as well as other words that start with an oddly narrow range of vowels. Inspiring! Educational! Invigorating! Enlightening!

Stop for a second. Can you think of a professional opportunity that you didn't take because your employer wouldn't pay for it?

I can't.

It hasn't always been smart, it hasn't always been prudent, and it hasn't always been successful. It hasn't even always been fun. But it has pushed me into the places I needed to be to move forward—on my own terms. Paying my own way has always been an investment in myself, and in my own power. When you take away their one reason for saying "no," then you are left with "yes."

This essay is not about how to save money. Throughout it, I may caution you to be way smarter about your finances than I was—do as I say, not as I did! Trust me on that. But mostly I will exhort you to spend your money, wisely, on yourself. Consider it an investment in your current career, next career, and general long-term marketability. I certainly do.

Okay! Hold on to your credit card and for God's sake don't break your 401(k). Here we go.

Go to the Story

Let's just agree that Aeroflot doesn't have the best airline safety record. Back in 2000, it wasn't any better. Yet on May 15, 2000, I found myself in the airport of Saint Petersburg, Russia, my expired visa in hand, bribing an airport official with whatever assortment of Swedish krona, Finnish marks, and Russian rubles I had in my pocket and purchasing a one-way ticket home to Stockholm on

Aeroflot—along with a goodly proportion of the Canadian hockey team.

I wasn't stalking the hockey team, not exactly. But you know when a big group of people who are supposed to be together hang out for a while in one place and the other random people hanging out near them start to look familiar and eventually become part of the group? That was me at the World Hockey Championships in 2000 at the Pribaltiyskaya Hotel in Saint Petersburg.

I was just finishing a six-month secondment at my law firm's Stockholm office, where a chance outing with the Canadian Club of Sweden to a Canada-Sweden hockey game had led to me befriending a goalie who told me about the championship tournament in May and said I should totally come. I totally agreed. I was a plucky but fairly clueless wannabe journalist with no actual contacts besides my pals from my college newspaper (the *Gazette* at the University of Western Ontario, holla!). I had been trying to place "only in Sweden!" stories from Stockholm, but was having little luck. Perhaps my beat could be "sports." Though a die-hard Canadian patriot, I had never been much for hockey until that moment, but the goalie convinced me that hockey was a sport worth watching (or, at the very least, was played by a strapping and manly bunch). I liked the chill of the air, the balletic power of players moving in tandem across the ice, watching my new goalie friend stop a puck going ninety miles an hour with just an outstretched glove. I liked his crooked-toothed smile, though I wasn't sure which teeth were actually his. Hockey can be dangerous.

Okay, so, to Russia I would go! I organized a group of girl-friends working and living in nearby cities into a posse (Sahra in Helsinki; Kati and Steph in Moscow; Sandra coming with me from Stockholm) and sleuthed out where the Canadian hockey team was staying to book us in that hotel, just to be near Canadians if anything untoward happened (I had never been to Russia; also, see above re: clueless). I bought a mini-tape recorder, loaded it up with film (this was 2000, people, my biggest expense by far was film and developing) and, crucially, ordered a guidebook called *The Girlfriend's Guide to Hockey* for an in-flight crash-course on hockey rules and history. I remember the author made lots of jokes about icing, as in, licking it off Mark Messier's chest. ("Icing" is when a player shoots the puck all the way across the ice, passing the center red line and the opposing team's goal line without being touched. You'd think that was the point, but no. Hockey is a game of rules and constraints, and if you can watch a game live on an Olympic-sized rink—from the stands, not some corporate box—you will find it dizzying, exhilarating, and wonderful. I promise.)

We arrived on day one at the Pribaltiyskaya Hotel (or "the Prib" as was more expedient to call it), which turned out to be a massive Soviet-era monolith with several in-house restaurants plus a bowl-ing alley. Thirteen out of the fourteen competing hockey teams were staying there (the Russians were sequestered to help their focus). Because of the timing, most teams boasted bona fide NHL players from teams that had already been eliminated from the playoffs. If you're a hockey fan you may recognize a few names from 2000: Jose Theodore of the Canadiens; Adrian Aucoin of the Senators; Todd Bertuzzi of the Canucks (as menacing in person as you'd think); Ed Jovanovski and Brendan Morrison of the Devils; Jamal Mayers of the Blues; the Sedin twins, newly draftable Swedish powerhouses; Kris Draper of the Red Wings, Phil Housley of the Sabres, and my hockey insta-crush Jeff Finley of the St. Louis Blues. The coaches included old-timers like 16-season NHL-er Butch Goring of the New York Islanders, famous for his four Stanley Cup wins and bat-tered helmet.

In addition to the players, the Prib was host to an international coterie of journalists, photographers, coaches, scouts, and members of the hockey cognoscenti, plus one supermodel. Carol Alt was there to cheer on her then-boyfriend (now husband) Alexei Yashin, sequestered away with the Russian team (alas, they were eliminated in the semis). I ran into her in the elevator and said, "bless you" when she sneezed, which was enough to ground a friendship, considering that she was surrounded by only hockey players and her boyfriend's mother, Tatiana. Carol had a limo at her disposal and would take our little gang of girls around town on her forays with Tatiana. Once, I joined her and Tatiana for a three-hour outing to the Russian Museum and for lunch afterward at a fancy hotel. Starving, I gratefully accepted a roll proffered by a waiter. Carol politely declined, informing me that bread was "toxic." Gulp. I left the roll untouched. I had a banana in my purse, and shortly thereafter, excused myself to the ladies' room to eat it. Protip: when out and about with supermodels, always keep a banana in your purse.

I developed my Russian routine. By day, the tournament, for which our gang would dress up in our national colors and cheer on our teams, quickly becoming a target of the TV cameras. (Why yes, that was me as #2 on Finnish TV's *Top Five Fans of the Game*.) By night, many of the aforementioned characters would gather at the second-floor bar for card-swapping, vodka-swilling, and tryst-planning with the friendly Russian ladies of the night who hung out in a banquette by the far back window. (I remember one named Katia, who quickly zeroed in on my goalie friend. Oh well. Back to focusing on work and trying not to openly gawk at Jeff Finley.) The second-floor bar became the place to be seen and to befriend, as well as to buy many rounds for people and then shut up and let them talk.

It's here that I will admit this was expensive. I was bankrolling the trip for me and Sandra, buying rounds of drinks, paying to attend the games, plus keeping plenty of cash on hand for hailing random cars as taxis, which apparently was the norm. I also had my hockey-nut law school friend Matt Meaghar on speed dial, and I'd call him regularly in Ottawa to decode some of the conversations and for general background. Once I lent my phone to a passel of players wanting to call home. Would I mind? Of course not! When I eventually got my phone bill, it was $2000. Worth it.

Canadian Press reporter Pierre LeBrun, who knew everything about hockey, the hockey scene, and its denizens, became one of my best friends at the Prib and would wave me over to the big groups of men clustered by affiliation (journalists, Canadians, coaches, and admins). Between my tattered little hockey book and my stealth lifeline back home, I quickly learned to hold my own in the group, refusing all offers of drinks and keeping my notebook prominent so they could tell I was a woman on the second floor for a specific professional purpose, not that other professional purpose. (This was important. One hockey player had come up to me in a group and, thinking I was Russian, said "Hey, chick with big tits!" I said, "Do you talk to your mother that way?" He said, "Whoops I thought you were a prostitute.")

Before I knew it, our week was over. There was still one more week of the tournament. Sandra was more than ready to return home; I was not. I hailed her a random car, stuffed some money in her hand, and assumed she'd get to the airport, then turned around to figure out where to stay for week two. With the foolhardiness of one who has never spent time in the Gulag, I forgot that my temporary Russian visa would soon expire, and decided to stay with my new friend Kati and booked a night at the Prib for the last night of the tournament, figuring that would be my last chance at a story. In the interim, I asked my new friend Carol to please store my giant pink suitcase, which I'd gotten for my bat mitzvah. She gladly agreed. As a thank-you, I got her a tin of caviar. Like I said, Russia was expensive.

Week two was an education. In week one, there were the de rigueur advances from horny hockey players; in week two, the wives and girlfriends showed up to leave us open-mouthed at just how brazen some of those dudes were. (Let the record reflect: as far as I was concerned, all stick-handling and goal-scoring was strictly limited to the ice.) My hockey journo friend Pierre, who had appointed himself my mentor, took me along to the Hermitage Museum on the free-day pilgrimage by the players; I can still remember what Jeff Finley's back looked like as he ambled along before me, ignorant of my presence. The days came and went, and Canada advanced further and further—yay!—but I had no sense of what my story was. I pinged my buddy Dave Feschuk, the former sports editor from the *Gazette*, now at the *Toronto Star*, and pitched him a story on the Prib itself, the international center of the hockey world that wasn't advancing to the playoffs toward the Stanley Cup. He passed it on to his editor, who said, "Okay, give me six hundred words right after the finals." Boom, it was real.

Canada had been knocked out in the semis, alas, but I was happy for the Czech Republic in their 5–3 defeat of Slovakia, and happy that it freed up even more players to speak to me, in English. I had three hours to turn the story around. Thank God for Pierre, for in this era before plentiful laptops and wireless devices, I was limited to the public terminals in the Prib, often competing with a bunch of burly players for screen time. (I caught one young Islander on a site called "Three's Cumpany." Charming.) Pierre had a laptop *and* a cable, and installed me in his room to pound out my story just under the wire. The headline: "Prib Becomes Paradise for Sports Fans." The billing? Sports section, page one, next to Pierre's Canadian Press wire piece. The accompanying photo? I kid you not: Jeff Finley.

The next day, the Team Canada bus gave me a lift to the airport, along with my giant pink suitcase, for which I was mocked. At the airport, the players wished me well as I appealed to the nice Russian official to overlook my expired visa. Then I followed the team to the

Aeroflot counter, thinking, if it's good enough for Team Canada, it's good enough for me. In theory, at least; the seats, which were covered in random, mismatched swatches of fabric, appeared to have been scavenged from other airplanes (this theory seemed borne out by the fact that I occupied seat 6D and the guy beside me was sitting in 10F). During the safety demonstration, the stewardess got tangled in the oxygen mask, and if there was an evacuation slide, I didn't know where it was, and if the stewardess knew, she wasn't telling, distracted as she was by the fact that her hands were now tied together. Team Canada was somewhere behind me, along with a cute hockey player who, if this plane went down, would die without knowing I existed. There was no escape from the fear except sleep, so that's what I did. I awoke midflight to find my head on the shoulder of the tolerant stranger beside me. I don't know what the word for "drool" is in Russian, but I think he forgave me.

Then suddenly, mercifully, bumpily, we were on the ground. So were the contents of my tray table, but why be picky? I was alive, I had my first national newspaper byline, and Carol Alt had almost cured me of bread. I said good-bye to my new friends as they went on to connect to their flight home to Canada and avoided eye contact with Jeff Finley, who I am sure never thought of me for a moment after, or really, before.

It was a crazy, expensive, ridiculous, expensive, semihazardous, expensive trip. But it brought me to the center of the story. It's also not an overstatement to say that it changed my life.

Accept Random Invitations—Especially the Ones No One Really Thinks You'll Accept

Let's fast-forward a few years. It's September 2005; and I am officially a freelance writer, one who has taught a few Mediabistro courses and started to speak on panels about how I left my job to be a journalist (those panels have since given way to how I left my job to start a start-up, but I digress). That first flag planted in the *National Post* sports section had led to several more sports "scene" stories—one about the tchotchkes sold at the U.S. Open, one about the scene on a bus to a Stanley Cup game (New Jersey Devils fans do love their jerseys). The Sports editor had introduced me to a colleague in the Life section, a lovely woman named Dianne de Fenoyl, and I migrated gratefully over there to pitch random stories like my law school friend's thirtieth birthday track-and-field party, a series on turning thirty (it was in 2002, sigh), and the infamous trip to Malta for the World Cup of Lawyers. (Pierre, meanwhile, had introduced me to his editor at the Canadian Press, and my first assignment was an interview with David Bowie, which I started on the plane and finished in a computer lab somewhere in Malta, transferred via a trusty floppy disk. 2002, I respect and am grateful for your technology.)

After earning a few clips in Canada, I was able to more credibly pitch myself here in New York, the city where I actually lived. I started to finagle bylines here and there, always conferring with my friends from my first Mediabistro writing course in 2002, including my pal Glynnis MacNicol. We hardly ever saw each other, but were in touch by e-mail, and it was good to have a friend to compare notes with as we went from total outsiders to clumsily groping our way in, ish. In 2004, I discovered the online magazine the Black Table and showed up to their summer roof party with a big bag of snacks and the pleading air of someone who really, really, wants you to like her.

Through my (unpaid) work at the Black Table, I met one of its founders, A. J. Daulerio, who recommended me for a job at a media blog working for Elizabeth Spiers, the founding editor of Gawker and the new editor in chief of Mediabistro. Though nothing came of that first meeting, in late March 2005, I got a panicky e-mail from her saying she had a sudden opening, and was I available immediately? By April 5, I was the new editor of FishbowlNY and a newly minted blogger. Elizabeth taught me how to blog on her personal blog. Publishing my first post the night before. So, onward.

The next eight months were a blur of round-the-clock obsession with the news cycle, the media, how the media was changing, and how I could bring it all back to show tunes. This wasn't my full-time job by a long shot—I made a $1500 honorarium per month—but I treated it like the only thing in my life. Some of the big stories at the time were the *Newsweek* Koran debacle, which was the first turn of the oil tanker that was the press pushing back against the Bush administration; the morning-show ratings rivalry between Katie Couric and Diane Sawyer; and Brian Williams starting a blog. There was another big story—the launch of the Huffington Post in May 2005.

Panned as an utter disaster before it was a full day old, the Huffington Post pushed everyone in media off-balance—who were these people on its front page spouting their opinions about the news? Steven Weber? Alec Baldwin? The highbrow journalism set sniffed; everyone else angled to get a spot on what had suddenly opened up as new online real estate. It was the mid-aughts and, for context, six months before the publication of Clive Thompson's seminal *New York* magazine story on the rise of blogging, which blared its importance from the cover via the hugely fonted word "Blog." Any new media property on the web was increasing the web's real estate by a significant factor.

I tracked it from my perch at my desk in my apartment on the Lower East Side, on my computer literally held together with a paper clip, staying up all night until the switch flipped and covering who was posting what and what everyone else was saying about it. Arianna seemed confident and glamorous as she blogged her blogs about blogging, and took hikes with fabulous women in media who tried to game out Judith Miller's source (2005!).

When Gawker founder Nick Denton invited me to a party he was hosting for Arianna at his fabulous Soho loft, I was ready. I pinged my ex-boyfriend Doug to be my date, because, sure, he was delightful company but he was also a former model. I asked my Greek friend Anastasia how to say "Welcome to New York!" in Greek. I bought a fancy red tube top from Velvet with strategically placed sequins that I thought was very sophisticated. (Oh, 2005. I think I miss your tube tops most of all.) I just wanted one minute with Arianna. Just so she could meet me, and know who I was.

The party was packed. Dougie, model-tall as well as handsome, scanned the crowd over everyone's head to find our quarry. There were always throngs of people between us and her. The speeches came and went. I started to quietly panic. I had one purpose there, one alone.

Suddenly she was coming toward us. I had my opening. "Hi Arianna. I'm Rachel Sklar from Fishbowl New York!" She was instantly warm with recognition, which I took to mean she'd recognized me. But you never know.

"Oh I looove Feeshbowl!" she said in her beautiful musical accent, and I fell instantly in love with everything about her, including her shiny hair. This was it. This was the time to make my mark. This was the time to speak Greek. "*Kalos orises! Ella* New York!" I said, obviously mangling the pronunciation as her brow furrowed. Panicked, I said the only other word in Greek that I knew. "*Malaka!*" I blurted, and her face went from shock to amusement, then laughter. If I am not mistaken, I had just called her a fucking masturbator. I would have launched something desperately into the pause that followed, but suddenly Nick Denton was swooping down on us. "Arianna! Have you met Jessica Coen?" Jessica was the talented, comely Gawker editor, and this party was basically meant for her. I bowed out gracefully, Dougie in tow. I remember nothing else from that night.

The next day in my blog recap,[1] I inserted an Easter egg: a sound file link to "Never On Sunday," which Anastasia had assured me was my closer. It was. Arianna e-mailed me how much she loved that song, and how nice it was to meet me. Protip: trust Greeks bearing gifts!

We stayed in touch. Later, she let me know she was having a party at her home in Los Angeles, for Nick, to return the favor. Would I be in town? "I would!" I said, and then booked a ticket.

Let's talk about money again for a minute: imagine the opposite of my cash-flush self making it rain in Saint Petersburg. I honestly could not have been more broke. I stayed at the cheapest of hotels and took the barest of taxi rides, opting to lug my giant suitcase around Santa Monica. (Finally, I had gotten rid of the pink one, but still, I like a big suitcase—I need options.) I settled on a sparkly little cream shrug from White House/Black Market to wear over my black—yes—tube top.

Arianna had suggested I come over early, and I had pitched an in-depth interview with her. She sent a car, and I luxuriated in the free ride to Brentwood—oh so free, so very, very free. We were having a glass of wine in the kitchen when Nick Denton walked in. I allowed myself to enjoy the look on his face. It was his party, but my point.

The party was great. The people were amazing. Bill Maher was there. David Mamet was there. I got to meet Megan Daum. There was a pool. There was food. I was there. Woot! Arianna was going to look after my ride home too and told me to stay till the end of the party, so we could talk further. I had my little recorder out. When everybody but a select few had left, we sat around and chatted some more before it was time for me to go. I left even more in love with her than before, and couldn't wait to go write up my superfun, superexclusive interview.[2]

And then I went home.

And then I quit Fishbowl.

And then Arianna and her partner Kenny Lerer offered me a job.

The day I accepted, she was on *The Colbert Report*, and I was invited to attend along with the staff. Afterward, she hugged me, put her hands on my shoulders, looked into my eyes, and said, "We're going to change the world."

I can tell you that paying my own way to Los Angeles for that party changed my life.

Bring Friends

Is there any adventure that is not made better by bringing a friend? Is there any skill that can't be complemented by a person you love and trust? Is there any long drive that can't be lightened by dancing to Icona Pop in the front seat or cracking up at goofy private jokes? Methinks not.

I have been so bloody lucky to have shared my random, wacky adventures with some amazing friends. With one friend in particular, I have traveled so much and covered so much ground that we've witnessed almost all of the sometimes incremental, sometimes exponential advancement of each other's careers. I could turn to her and say "Welcome, Wolf Blitzer!" and it would instantly crack her up. It just cracked me up. If he understood the context, I think it might even crack Wolf Blitzer up.

That person is my friend Glynnis MacNicol, now my cofounder at TheLi.st, with whom I have shared two primaries, three White House Correspondents' dinners, four political conventions, and umpteen hotel room beds (and one very comfortable single-person air mattress at the 2008 DNC). Glynnis and I graduated from e-mail friends to air-mattress-sharing friends by way of my recruiting her to HuffPo as an associate media editor in early 2007. She quickly became my closest sounding board, party partner, and 2008 presidential election debate co-live-blogger, which actually meant we spent an unholy number of nights together tethered to our TVs and computers over pizza. This is how great friendships are born.

With an insane election schedule, 2008 went straight from New Year's into Iowa to New Hampshire then a swing south and into the Super Tuesday blitz. If you don't remember what the lead-up to the 2008 election was like, allow me to remind you. It was insane. The well-oiled Hillary locomotive was barreling forward on an inevitable collision course with the newer, shinier Obama train. Somewhere on the tracks was John Edwards. And then of course there was the throng of white men vying for the Republican nomination, hoping there was a chance that Rudy Giuliani could still be edged out as front-runner.

I wanted in. This was the biggest story that I'd ever been part of, and HuffPo was in the middle of it, right along with the rest of the media. I had been living and breathing election news for months, writing voraciously, appearing regularly on TV as a political pundit, my social life consisting pretty much exclusively of professional events. In 2008, they were taking the party on the road. I had to go with.

I drafted a long memo to the HuffPo brass, explaining why their crack media blogger should join the road trip too. Alas, the budget could only support members of the newly minted politics team—we were still a start-up; unfortunately it wasn't feasible at this time.

The FOMO (fear of missing out) was intense. Not going wasn't an option, and to be honest, it never occurred to me. New Hampshire was a five-hour bus ride from New York. I—we—would go anyway.

Of course Glynnis was coming. By this time, she was at my old stomping ground, FishbowlNY, which had no budget either. So we booked ourselves into an Econo Lodge—fancy!—and assessed our options. One of them was to ride on a bus of Hillary supporters as improvised "embedded" journalists, and voilà! A few bus interviews and some hand-coding on my BlackBerry, and I'd filed my first story before we'd even crossed the state line.[3]

Everything about the trip was either exhilarating, hilarious, scary, or all three. The scene was exhilarating—you couldn't cross the floor of the Radisson in Manchester without tripping over a candidate (Mitt Romney), a news anchor (Brian Williams), or a phalanx of young reporters headed to the bar (Ryan Lizza, Kelly O'Donnell, Michael Crowley). The Econo Lodge was hilarious, best explained by this anecdote: one night as we were being dropped off by a male colleague at our hotel, a cop stopped us because he assumed that we were prostitutes. (I do not know why this has been a running theme.)

The spin room following the 2008 New Hampshire debate was scary, with the swirling mass of old and new media jockeying for an angle and the scrums of each candidate bumping up against each other, with flashbulbs popping and boom mics overhead and famous pundits clustered together to cement the conventional wisdom of the moment. (One pundit who shall remain nameless shouted me down for saying the "You're likeable enough, Hillary" exchange was notable, and instead asserted that Hillary's take on energy efficiency would be the takeaway moment. Uh-huh.) This was where it was important to have a friend by your side, not just to pinch you as you say, "Is that Hendrik Hertzberg?" but also to be there when you are suddenly assailed by imposter syndrome, panic, and try to flee. Someone to say, "No way. We belong here as much as anyone."

We rented a car and drove around to various events (this is another good reason to bring friends—I don't have my driver's license). We saw a Huckabee jamboree live; caught the infamous "Iron My Shirt!" moment at a Hillary rally as it happened; popped onto the Straight Talk Express (McCain's bus) when we couldn't get into a McCain rally; and posted photos and blog pieces throughout the day. This was before Twitter had taken hold of mainstream media, so if you were blogging, you were at the forefront of real-time news. Just by being on-site I was able to wrangle myself a TV hit on *Morning Joe*, one on CBC to say hi to the folks back home, plus all manner of interviews, including one with Romney spokesperson Kevin Madden, who became a friend and my go-to guy so I could say, "Look! I'm friends with Republicans!" On the last day, my HuffPo colleague Sam Stein, one of the precious few funded politics writers, was out a hotel room and needed a place to crash. I said sure—and the Econo Lodge welcomed one more denizen (actually, two—the *Nation*'s Ari Berman was crashing with him).

All told, our room had housed me, Glynnis, our friend Sophie, our other friend Sven, Sam, Ari, and our makeshift mobile newsroom and editing suite (for digital camera interviews, of course). The Econo Lodge was for everyone . . . but Sam paid for that night.

When the time came for the 2008 Conventions, it wasn't even a question: we were going. HuffPo was able to cover my flights— huge!—but hotel rooms had been booked solid for months by news organizations with travel departments, and any stray options were far away from the main action and wildly expensive. There was, however, craigslist! (Remember, there was once a time before Airbnb.) With luck and obsessive searching, I found us a sweet one-bedroom condo and struck a deal with a friend whose company would pay for most of it if she got the room. Perfect! We'd bed down on the floor in the living room. That friend was Amber Ettinger, aka Obama Girl. Not the worst wing-woman to have at the 2008 Democratic National Convention.

We were about a block from downtown Denver, convenient and walkable to all venues, including the convention center—a score, based on the reaction of colleagues grumbling about having to stay a few miles out of town. One of those people was Craig Newmark, whom we bumped into early in our stay. He was complaining about his location and we bragged to him about our sweet condo. How'd we get it? he asked. It was pretty fun to say, "Craigslist!"

When I think of the highlights of my career, I think of the 2008 DNC. The collision of the excitement around Obama with the sudden proliferation of accessible media tech (blogging, digital cameras, and smartphone photos—and, crucially, Twitter) meant an explosion of content, events, and opportunities to create and contribute to both. New media suddenly had cachet, which meant we were included on every invitation to mix with all levels of people. (Fun fact: this photo of me with Jon Hamm was used as his Wikipedia photo for about two years thereafter, though, of course, I was understandably cropped out. I would have done the same.[4]) The access was astounding, the learning curve skyrocketing, the opportunity tremendous.

If you wrote about politics and media, you had to be there. So when I learned that my friend Ana Marie Cox, then at *Time*'s Swampland blog, was not coming, I e-mailed her immediately, telling her to join us in our gonzo coverage adventure: "Hop a flight to Denver and stay with us! It will be tight but who cares—it will also be hilarious. Get on a plane, the rest is actually a lot easier to figure out than really it should be."

She did. So instead of Glynnis taking the couch and me taking the single-person air mattress, we gave Ana the couch and shared. I don't remember being uncomfortable, cranky, tired, or otherwise anything but delighted with my sleeping arrangements. In fact, it led to the only sort-of viral video I've ever been part of—an impromptu morning "vlog" (back when people would unironically use the word "vlog") featuring the three of us nestled in bed together, commenting on the previous night's speeches on the convention floor. It was

cozy but truly fun, and I still stand by our sharp, insightful punditry, as well as my impressively steady camera arm.[5]

Ana filed some terrific pieces from both the DNC and the RNC,
and her presence made the whole thing that much more fun—and
professionally rewarding—for me and Glynnis. Remember that
thing about bringing friends? It also works for making them.

Here was the other lesson of my whirlwind 2008 adventures in
political reporting: I belonged there. I had credentials around my
neck, a smartphone in my hand, and *work* to do. Yes it was fun, but
that was because I loved the work. It was the reason I was there and
the reason why it didn't matter how I was paying for it. I may not
have been at the stage of travel departments or chauffeured town
cars or signs with my name waiting for me at airports, but I was
there, and part of it. I didn't need a sign at an airport to tell me I was
in the right place. It was enough just to see one that said "Welcome,
Wolf Blitzer!"

Like all news organizations, HuffPo had a budget. That's fine. I
respected that and still do. I may not be in control of their budget,
but I'm in control of my own—and it was 100 percent worth it
to me to invest in my own experience, professional development,
relationships, and, frankly, good time. I never went on spring break
to Daytona Beach, but 2008 on the campaign trail felt plenty wild
enough.

Book the Ticket There. You'll Find a Way Home

I'm going to come back to money now. Just for a second. In your
life, you will likely experience times when you are the one with
money and your friends are struggling. You will also likely experience times when your friends are the ones ordering surf and turf
washed down by bottles of fine wine while you're filling up on water
and free bread, praying that no one will say, "Oh, let's just split the

check." Real friends bring lots to the table, and your life is much better when they're by your side.

Let's extrapolate to the business world. Some professionals are much better resourced than others. If you can share a paid-for hotel room, do it. If you can pick up dinner on your corporate card with your per diem, do it. If you can expense that car rental, parking fee, gas refill, taxi, late-night room service—do it. Don't think twice about how lopsided it might feel. Consider it an investment in possibility, in who-knows-where-things-might-end-up-going.

In September 2010, I was invited at the last minute to speak at TechCrunch Disrupt in San Francisco, on the first-ever (and only since) women-in-tech panel.[6] The invitation was triggered by a comment I'd made about the abysmal gender ratio at the conference. Because the comment had been in the *Wall Street Journal*, it got some attention, and, after a few flame-war blog posts and a comment insurrection, TechCrunch convened this last-minute panel and invited me to be on it.

I was as broke as I have ever been, but I knew I had to go. Here is how I made that happen: (1) Traded a friend's air miles for cash (less cash than the cheapest ticket). (2) Now out of cash, borrowed a hundred bucks from my ex-boyfriend, so I could cover cabs to and from airports. (3) Arranged to crash with my friend Ashley Granata, the cofounder of fashion-tech start-up Fashism, who I'd gotten into the conference as my plus one. She knew I was hurting, so she picked up my half of the room, saying she knew it would come back to her (it did). While I was in San Francisco, an automatic deposit to my bank account came through, which was how I bought my plane ticket home.

Was that a stressful few days? Yes. Was it imperative for me to be there? Turns out, yep. Should you do that? I don't know. I just want you to know that you have the option, that it's possible, and that investments in yourself are worth what you pay for them.

Okay, Now Go Put Some Money in Savings

Writing this essay has been a delight. I loved remembering where I was, where I wanted to be, and how fun—and hard—it was to get there. It helped me appreciate how much work we put into our own selves, how much fear and sweat and risk and pain and *tsuris*, what the Jews call that combination of worry and anxiety that makes you reach for the Maalox and Pepto with both hands.

It also makes me realize how terrible a negotiator I was for myself. I'm glad I *did* pay my own way, but for many of my self-funded trips, I should not have had to. What I know now is that, in addition to compensation, I should have negotiated for my own development and ability to participate fully in the sphere of my daily professional whirl. I should not have paid for SXSW when I went representing Mediaite. (Or, for that matter, the White House Correspondents' dinner when I went representing Mediaite.) But in your professional life, as in all of life, things are not always fair.

So when someone tells you "no" and refuses to look out for you, I'm here to tell you that is not your only option. You have an alternative: drain your bank account, grab a friend, and know it will come back to you.

And either way, you are allowed to eat bread.

Notes

1. Rachel Sklar, "Denton Drinks for Arianna: Everybody Wang Chung on Wednesday, Everybody Hurts on Thursday," *FishbowlNY*, September 23, 2005, https://www.mediabistro.com/fishbowlny /denton-drinks-for-arianna-everybody-wang-chung-on-wednesday -everybody-hurts-on-thursday_b1087.

2. Rachel Sklar, "Arianna Huffington: Politics, Punditry and the HuffPo Family," *FishbowlNY*, February 6, 2006, http://www.mediabistro.com/fishbowlny/arianna-huffington-politics-punditry-and-the-huffpo-family_b1661.

3. Glynnis MacNicol and Rachel Sklar, "What Happens in Iowa Stays in Iowa: Hillary's Cavalry Rides to the Rescue," *Huffington Post*, January 4, 2008, http://www.huffingtonpost.com/glynnis-macnicol-and-rachel-sklar/what-happens-in-iowa-stay_b_79915.html.

4. Rachel Sklar's Flickr site, August 28, 2008, http://www.flickr.com/photos/rachelsklar/3011533686/in/photostream. Photo of Jon Hamm (and me!).

5. "The Ana Marie Cox—Glynnis MacNicol—Rachel Sklar Morning Show," *Guest of a Guest*, August 28, 2008, http://guestofaguest.com/new-york/politics/the-ana-marie-cox-glynnis-macnicol-rachel-sklar-morning-show.

6. "Women In Tech," Transcript from panel at TechCrunch Disrupt SF on September 28, 2010, posted by Rachel Sklar on Medium, March 14, 2014, https://medium.com/p/51af6ef51e27.

9.
A CULTURE OF EXTRAORDINARY

Stacy London

You may or may not know that I spent ten years on a TV show or that I wrote some books or that I did some other stuff. But I can tell you I spent the last ten years of my life without ever looking up. That isn't bragging; it's an admission. I was going so fast for so long, I didn't even know the velocity at which I was operating. As a trained stylist who had worked in magazines for many years, the opportunity to be on television was an exciting but certainly, I assumed, a short-lived one. This assumption was based on two things: that the window of opportunity on something as out of the blue as this would close quickly, and two, that I had no experience in television. Little did I know that one thing would lead directly into another. I quickly discovered that my skill for styling *and* my skill for communicating *and* a penchant for ad-lib would propel my career forward because television really was the best medium for me to use and highlight those skills in a unique, authentic way.

But after ten years, my full-time stint on TV has come to an end and for the first time, I have not accelerated the pace of my life but decelerated it. It is the first time I have "looked up." I have spent my life becoming a career woman and being a self-sufficient one at that. (Mom was a frontline feminist.) Let's face it; we all deserve a rest at some point. The funny thing about rest is that people don't know exactly what to say to you. There is usually a pause of some kind, just a beat or two, before a reply. Some have overly agreed with me that I need a break; some stare in disbelief; some take it as an opportunity to tell me all their problems. And it is the first time I have wondered whether some of this dismay doesn't stem directly from the shift in our culture to always being "on," and that taking time "off" doesn't even make sense in a world of instant connectivity.

I realize that taking a rest takes a certain amount of resolve on my part. When one has access all day long to text and Twitter and Facebook, Instagram and Pinterest (I haven't even gotten to Snapchat yet), it can quickly feel like what you have accomplished isn't enough to stand (still) on. To wake up and look around at a world so very different from the one I entered when I started television has been startling. Now, everyone thinks they should be on TV. That is not to say that our society hasn't always put a certain amount of value in the concept of fame but now, the desire for it seems to have grown in direct proportion to the ease with which one can acquire attention. To have "more" when it comes to almost anyone is to be more known, more recognized, indeed, more famous. The bar of notoriety has been lowered since I started in television. You don't actually need any kind of expertise; you just need to be notice-able: beautiful, funny, crazy, etc. And for that, you are quantifiably rewarded with hearts and retweets. Of course, in a world where housewives and Kardashians are idolized, I can see how TV actually set the precedent.

With the help of social media, we can all be celebrities to some extent. The reason past achievements feel like they matter less is because, in a real sense, they do. If they aren't constantly being revamped, reorganized, and restated, our achievements and our skills seemingly have less value because repetition in the face of immediacy is virtual death. It is the failure to keep your viewer, your consumer, your fan engaged. Somewhere in the past ten years, the pace of content creation has replaced the quality of the content. It no longer seems to matter if it's good or helpful or valuable. It just has to come out constantly. Because if you don't have anything new to say (or a new way to say the same thing), go ahead and make some shit up. Who will know the difference?

In the world of style, this is an increasingly difficult obstacle. When I started my career in print magazines, fashion was an exclusive world. Only editors went to fashion shows and knew what the trends would be six months later. We would get to see the latest fashions only when the magazines came out each month. The editors were the experts (partially because they had knowledge we as the public were not privy to) and print was the medium of their power. Then came the advent of reality television, and I have said before, shows like *What Not To Wear*, *Queer Eye for the Straight Guy*, and *Project Runway* shone a light onto the inner workings of an exclusive, notoriously snobby field.

When I started in TV, it was the era of learning that things you aspired to (a nice home, good style) were not outside the realm of possibility any longer. *Trading Spaces* and *While You Were Out* showed us *how* to furnish our lives, and style programs showed us *how* we could dress without having to be skinny, rich, or young. Reality television burst in the door and introduced you to experts who were there to help *you*. But the how-to advice of television is no longer a necessity. How-to is a click, not a day away. And while there are kajillions of TV channels, there are a kajillion more digital outlets. Now, you can watch a fashion show live-streamed *as* Anna Wintour is watching it. Anyone, everyone (including Ms. Wintour) can be his or her own brand of expert because immediacy of information disallows for exclusivity of that information.

The fact is, being on TV somehow gives people a halo of authority; they were not picked by accident. Someone decided they could be authoritative and entertaining and gave them a platform. By comparison in the digital world, everyone is an expert not only by what they say but how often they say it. They are not chosen by the few, they become respected by the many. Reality television "experts" gave birth to the modern day blogger. In this new world order, you can interact with your idols directly and you can gain power and expert status by creating a following.

TV experts, real or fake, only had to supply content, at most, once a day. And, at most, in print once a month. In social media, one can post content once a minute. Is it possible to supply good, even great, content that quickly? I don't know but I don't think so. I suppose it depends on how you value that content. It is undeniable that you can gain a greater audience and create a bigger fan base by submitting any kind of content. At least that seems to be the trick. The same thing that made a TV show successful is the same thing that makes an online star or a brand successful: engagement. However, social media has changed how to get and keep someone's attention because our attention has been molded by the medium itself.

I woke up after my ten years on TV and now the number of Instagram followers one has seems to determine one's worth, both personally and commercially. We live in an extraordinary time. Louis C.K. talks about how we forget and overlook the miracles of flying at thirty thousand feet in huge hunks of metal, of communicating through wireless phones. And our kids (well, not mine) can take cough syrup that tastes like bubble gum. We live in an age of extreme development and evolution. To be clear, all ages have been full of development and evolution, but what seems most interesting is how a change in pace and advances in technology have actually, literally, changed our interactions with each other and the way we value those interactions, indeed, each other's worth.

Everyone is in it to win it. Everything moves at the speed of a tweet. If you can't keep up, sometimes it feels as though what came before this moment is not only past, it is not even important. To someone whose career meant being on once a week in someone's living room, the necessity to reach people *all* the time on this level is an acutely foreign and uncomfortable one. I don't want to share *everything*. Call me selfish. It's all a bit strange to me, like having a pocket full of francs in the age of the euro. When I give fashion advice, I say it once and it's meant to stick.

In print and TV, advice doesn't come as often but comes with a certain amount of validity based on prior experience. Wear dark-colored jeans to slim your thighs. The advice doesn't change because *it works*. But how do we impart information, helpful or otherwise, when the need for new information changes so quickly and there is so much of it out there? It is a time in which what one did yesterday will be bested or contradicted by what someone else does today. Or three hours from now. Where does the authenticity of information come from?

I am literally awed by bloggers who post ten times a day and astounded by huge Internet giants like *HuffPo*, Yahoo!, and AOL who, with all their divisions, tweet some piece of content every thirty seconds. (It's worth noting that AOL actually has a division called AOL On. I follow them on Twitter, natch.) The fact that good information retains its value is now a handicap. In order to be an online expert/celebrity, *more* information has more value. Constancy is the hallmark of expertise, not the content itself.

My point here isn't actually to say I don't belong in this Brave New World any more or less than anyone else, but arriving late to the party has given me a bit of perspective: we are a civilization that exceeds at excess. We consistently hold ourselves to such exhausting standards that it is easy to lose confidence in who we are. We, as a culture, have a deep-seated need to be liked, validated, and prized, even to the point of being willing to turn the most mundane or the most private of things into grist for the digital mill. And the demands of social media have reinforced this cultural neurosis even further.

I am beginning to wonder if we've become more unabashed about our behavior, not because we are any freer or less judgmental as a society but because any attention is now good enough to posit a claim of expertise and a bid for celebrity. Perhaps in this day and age, we can't appreciate the talents we do possess unless we feel they have been acknowledged by an "audience." There is no immediate reciprocity in print (or TV for that matter). Magazines know they are doing well by circulation numbers and maybe a few letters to the editor. Television shows know their ratings the following day. It's no wonder media giants like Condé Nast, Hearst, and Time Inc. have upped their game online or that networks are all now scrambling for second screen engagement.

As a parallel, I have written and spoken many times about the unrealistic nature of advertising for women. Use this shampoo and you'll look like a model, use this moisturizer and look twenty years younger. Buy this lingerie so you are sexy. And on and on. We buy in to the hype of these products, consciously or unconsciously. And we want what they offer because we are looking for confirmation: confirmation that we are beautiful, confirmation that we are loved, confirmation that we can swing our hair back and forth (props to Willow Smith here) and be confident in who we are.

But we are also faced with many other standards of extraordinary that may not be as easily identified. Since the feminist revolution, women have achieved a greater sense of equality and freedom, but there has also been a price to pay for it. (And while

Obama's recent State of the Union address spoke a lot about women and the right to equal pay, even the right to stay home with a sick child and not lose one's job, there is still more.)

There has been some fallout, even failure, from that revolution of forty years ago. In some ways, it has set us adrift, and the standards we hold ourselves to are just as unrealistic as looking like Gisele. We are meant to do, have, and be it all: everything to everyone. We should be financially (and even emotionally) independent because we have proved we can be single mothers and raise children, because we can have sex out of wedlock, because we can ascend to boardrooms and CEO offices. Because we can bring home the bacon, fry it up in a pan, with or without a man. And we're supposed to do it with a perfect body, a killer dress sense, a fresh mani-pedi, a blowout, *and* a smile, obvi. We'll go to spin class at six a.m. and be at work on time. We'll get to our child's recital *and* fund-raise for the latest charity.

The effect of all of this self-sufficiency is an exhausting scenario, which we have painted for ourselves. If we act like superheroes, people are apt to believe we are ones. And if we never act as if we need help, quiet, privacy, or intimacy, it seems very logical that we won't get it. And worse, if we make ourselves believe we can be superheroes, our insecurities are made worse when there is some inevitable failure.

Now, rather than just feeling as if we are attempting to do all these things and be all these things, for friends and family, we are meant to seem as if we are all succeeding by playing all of them out on the much larger public platform of social media. This is the age of personal branding and everyone is a star. It is no longer as simple as dressing ourselves well and baking cookies or nailing a deal; it is proving how clever we are, how much fun we are, how busy we are, how witty we are, even how vulnerable we are. This is the ta-da jazz-hands moment, and this is something you need to create ten times a day, every day. You don't just have to be the woman who does everything; you now have to *show* that you are (even if you aren't). Welcome to the new résumé.

Wearing a fabulous outfit isn't solely about empowerment. It isn't simply a tool for telling the world what you want to say about yourself. It's only true if you have the likes to prove it. Not only are we holding ourselves to unreasonable standards in life, but we are now competing for brand recognition through actual scores. Back in the prehistoric pre-Internet days, TV personalities were assessed with Q ratings—how audiences responded to them on a variety of levels—but it was an industry-only system. Social media has done away with the need for ANY specific industry system. You are the number of followers you have and that makes you and your brand's "worth" quantifiable; TV personality or teenager, it makes no difference. The social media game is one big popularity contest based on the amount of content posted, in the shortest amount of time. It is never enough to do something, write something, or say something once and have it be noticed, countered, respected, or retained. Repetition is the only way to stay immediate, and this constant engagement is kinda . . . (HELLO?) . . . exhausting.

I experienced some degree of fame in a postfeminist pre-Internet age, and perhaps that is why I experience such a sense of confusion (even anxiety) over this digital one. Sharing constantly feels like oversharing to me. Total transparency is the new black. And the burden of constantly sharing seems to add exponentially to an already exhausting culture. Even as a reality show personality, I am someone whom people feel they know intimately. I still feel somewhat uncomfortable with the idea that my private time isn't always respected. People feel they can come up to me when I'm on the phone or at dinner with my family and interrupt like we are old pals. People sometimes mistake that because I was in an unscripted show, they knew exactly who I was as a person. One woman actually yelled at me on the street for wearing sneakers. (I was going to the gym.) But that familiarity is exactly what Internet fame seems to invite, perhaps insists on. Rather than make a line in the sand, it blurs the existence of personal and public altogether, making room for a new kind of inauthentic intimacy, authority, and recognition. Being aware of people and their activities to this extent, one can easily and quickly establish a categorical relationship with them.

As much as audiences might think that seeing and hearing me speak unscripted words is the same as knowing me, it is only in that particular context and only a part of me: a style expert giving advice. Watching every single episode of *What Not To Wear* would not tell you who I am. But the "masters of the digital universe" have based their brands on *who they are*. Or at least, who they want us to think they are. The expectation of intimacy is even greater because these people are asking, actually inviting, you to live their lives with them, to share their experience as often as possible. It is a whole new level of TMI. I'm not saying for everyone, but certainly for me, this age of transparency and quippy taglines on Instagram grew up around me when I wasn't paying all that much attention. I certainly have never been "brand conscious" about my tweets. I never thought I needed to be.

This isn't even about fame or brands exclusively. Perhaps the reason this is of such interest to me is because the way we dress; how much we can handle and how well we multitask; how many people are watching and clapping their hands as we "dive"; even how many followers we have is all essentially about the same thing: the presentation of ourselves to the world versus who we actually are. And while I have always said and believed that presentation is important, its value changes when we are no longer aware of it as a presentation. The immediacy with which we engage one another online creates such a fascinating scenario: Is it organic connection or wholly artifice? Is it helpful or hurtful to the generations who have never experienced the difference? Isn't an achievement still an achievement, even when no one's looking?

This appears to be the time when we examine the line between where we have been and where we are going. I question whether the immediacy of social media makes our need for recognition and validation no longer about those few who truly know and love us, but about the masses that don't. Are transparency and constancy the ingredients of what authenticity looks like? Self-deprecation and sharing moments that were once considered private has suddenly become the new currency of honesty. In an effort to be more popular, are we trading in who we are for who our audience wants us to be? Is controlling one's image online any different than having a publicist in real life or keeping your addiction to the zooborns.com a secret? (Oh come *on*, you already knew that about me.)

As Lena Dunham so interestingly said in a recent *Vogue* article:

I have a really great private existence, almost more like a memoirist or a columnist would, and less like an actor would," she says. "Which I enjoy, because I can't overstate how much I hate leaving the house." Dunham sees her apartment as an extension of herself: She couldn't undertake bold feats of self-disclosure in public—the stories of her sexual history, the portraits of her family life, the nakedness—if she didn't have it to return to. "No one would describe me as a private person, but I actually really am," she explains. "It's important for me to have a lot of time alone, and to have a lot of time in my house by myself. My entire life sort of takes place between me and my dog, my books, and my boyfriend, and my private world. To me, privacy isn't necessarily equated with secret-keeping. What's private is my relationship with myself.[1]

There is a particular and intentional genius to Lena Dunham. Everyone can relate to the new kind of antiheroine she puts out there. But one might suggest that her true brilliance is in getting people to identify so wholly with a persona she is not solely. Creating the appearance of authenticity both on a scripted TV series and by taking and posting pictures on Instagram of her boyfriend, her dog, her so-called life, is an intentional and crafted exercise in supposed intimacy. We think we know the real her. But this quote would suggest just the opposite. While she did not begin her career with an Instagram account, and she possesses talent with or without social media, she has simply become accustomed to the technology of her age. Rather than being a talent because of the technology of her age. She has harnessed its power to her advantage.

People just ten years younger than I have grown up within the culture of social media. They appear to say who they are in 140 characters. They understand they are their brand profiles, and they recognize the necessity of the constant renewal of content in ways that completely elude me and the world from which I came. They are always on or ready to be. They remember to document *everything*. Their eyes are open to every possibility of a new post. (Taking a kajillion selfies of myself in my forties just feels weird. But hey, Oprah makes Instagram videos, like, every *day*. So clearly she has the hang of this.) Does the measure of being good at something now require an audience to prove it? What if what you're posting isn't really good at all? Who decides? She with the most followers wins? Is Instagram instaconnection or instavalidation or instabullshit?

Seriously, if I don't take a picture of my salad to post online, does that mean I didn't eat it? Without likes, can't I still enjoy it? I am only half kidding. Because if the picture of my salad with a "Lo-Fi" filter looks better than the actual salad, at least I've created the illusion that I had something even more wonderful than the reality of it. And now, I have proof of a fake perfection I can't replicate in real life.

There is a new faith in instainfluence. Yet the actual meaning of the quantifiable metrics remains to be determined. I can buy five thousand followers on Twitter tomorrow. If a twelve-year-old has two million followers, should she be given a cosmetics contract? Maybe. Just asking. Increase immediacy and availability over time, one begins to question legitimacy. Not every single person with an opinion can garner the same number of viewers. Eventually, those with something particular and special will rise to the top. Digital media insists, however, they can't stay there. The speed of content production and reinvention disallows for the time it takes to appreciate talent or expertise. Which brings me back around to the question: To accomplish something, must there be an audience to validate it? Can't a woman be an amazing mother without being a mommy blogger? So many great achievements have taken place in history with and, more to the point, without recognition. Social media recognizes everyone. So if everyone gets a medal, is everyone "#winning?"

This feels like a tectonic shift in terms of our cultural, collective experience, a truly extraordinary one. My generation (X, by the way) may be the last to even notice it. This shift is similar to the long, hard fight of feminism, but it may be that we have burdened ourselves with even more unrealistic expectations. Do social media and influence set us up to value attention and recognition more than achievement? Or is digital engagement the latest skill we need to learn in order to feel as if we've achieved more and appear more than we actually are?

Honestly, I don't know whether we've raised or relaxed the cultural expectations of achievement in this viral age. The game is open to all, and the playing field is level. (As long as you can be funny in 140 characters or less.) But the competition feels no less intense from where I'm standing. Perhaps by allowing everyone the chance to brand themselves publicly, we diversify the ideals of our society. Perhaps by becoming the new voices of the next generations, sharing (even everything) is the next stage of feminism: to rid ourselves of secrets and hiding and shame and any sort of inequality? Or do we simply enter into a more savage display of one-upmanship?

Do we purposely hide (or show) all our flaws and idiosyncrasies in favor of a range of filter options? Are we just trading in an old set of insecurities for another—fear of missing out (FOMO) instead of good old-fashioned envy? Are we faulted for not putting it all out there, for wanting privacy and a life separate from the one we show online or anywhere else? Or by its very nature, is it never possible to show who one truly is because our personas are constructed and controlled? Perhaps our biggest error is believing in our own hype.

Lately I've been told repeatedly that my livelihood depends in part on my online engagement. Having been a host on TV for ten years does not hold the same value it once did. Having two million followers on a social media platform does. Frankly, some days I'm not sure I'm up to the challenge. Will the skills that made me successful on television serve me at all on another media platform? Will the skills of social media stars serve them anywhere else? I suppose we'll all have to wait and see.

In some ways, technology allows for a new sense of intimacy and autonomy. I get that. Rather than be *told* what to do by experts, we *share* what we do with the people we identify with. Experts (even celebrities) come down off their pedestals and share their flaws, faults, and what it means to be human. We have access to each other like never before. Access breeds familiarity, so as a brand it is essential to remain in contact with your audience, not simply for recognition but for that essential sense of intimacy and identification so necessary to fostering loyalty.

In no way is this essay meant to be an attack on the progression of technology. I am mostly just amazed by the speed with which this has all happened. It's like watching the gentrification of a neighborhood at warp speed. The general public used to rely on the expertise of those in a specific field. Now, it seems, people will heed advice from just about anyone whose experience is reflective of theirs and with whom they can establish an open line of communication. Is this due to the immediacy and, at least seeming, intimacy of the digital age? What happens when the amount of information becomes so endless that googling "How to tie a scarf" won't bring up fifty websites, but five million?

I would argue that if we become paralyzed by the myriad choices in front of us, the need for experts, or at least aggregators, becomes important and relevant once again. So I humbly predict that there will be shifts. With all the people branding themselves, we'll eventually need people to help us navigate these choices. There will always be voices that rise above the others. Those people may be viewed and valued as experts once again and the playing field will change. I wouldn't be surprised if digital magazines become the leaders in information: print, reimagined. And I won't be surprised if how-to TV comes back into style when audiences are fed up with women having plastic surgery and throwing tables just to stir shit up. You will have heard it here first, people.

I'm reminded that this essay is included in a compilation entitled *The 10 Habits of Highly Successful Women*. I haven't really presented a habit here. But perhaps there is a habit implicit in this essay: you will always have to do the work of interpreting and validating information for yourself, from any source. As well as the work of discerning what is immediate and changeable with information that remains intact across all mediums. All of which should give the hashtag #nofilter an entirely new meaning.

Notes

1. Nathan Heller, "Lena Dunham: The New Queen of Comedy's First Vogue Cover," *Vogue*, January 15, 2014, http://www.vogue.com /magazine/article/lena-dunham-the-new-queen-of-comedys-first-vogue-cover.

10.

CHANGING THE WORLD THROUGH BUSINESS AND SEX: THE FIVE THINGS I LEARNED THAT COULD HELP YOU TOO

Cindy Gallop

Changing the world through business and sex" might sound odd, but I believe it's entirely possible.

How It All Began

I date younger men—usually in their twenties (I'm fifty-four). Which is how I began encountering, six or seven years ago, an issue that would never have crossed my mind if I had not come across it directly and intimately: what happens when total freedom of access to hard-core porn online meets our society's equally total reluctance to talk openly and honestly about sex, resulting in porn becoming, by default, the sex education of today—in not a good way.

The average age today at which a child first views hard-core porn online is eight.[1] A global study conducted by BitTorrent earlier this year indicates that children as young as six are exposed to online porn.[2] This isn't because eight-year-olds and six-year-olds go looking for porn. It's a function of what they're shown on someone's cell phone at the playground; what happens when they go to a neighbor's house—because it doesn't matter what parental controls you have at home, your kids live their lives in other places. Or, because this is the most wired generation ever, an eight-year-old does something cute and innocent: they learn a new naughty word, they google it—Penis! Hee hee!—and one or two clicks away is something they never expected to find.

That's why the *New York Times* ran an article in 2012 called "So How Do We Talk About This? When Children See Internet Pornography."[3]

And that's why, as I discovered for myself in my own dating life years before the media began frenziedly covering this issue, young men and women who grow up today, watching hard-core porn online for years before they ever have their own first romantic or sexual experiences, assume that what they see in porn is what sex is and that it is how you do it for real.

"Pro-sex. Pro-porn. Pro-knowing the difference."
I found myself encountering a number of, shall we say, sexual behavior memes, and thought, *Whoa! I know where that behavior's coming from, and if I'm experiencing this, lots of other people must be as well.* I'm a naturally action-oriented person, and so I decided to do something about it. Five years ago I conceived, built, and launched (on no money, which is why it's so clunky and basic) makelovenotporn .com, which posts the myths of hard-core porn and balances them with reality—"Porn World" versus "Real World"—in a straightforward, nonjudgmental, humorous way.

It's important to note that MakeLoveNotPorn is not antiporn. Our tagline is "Pro-sex. Pro-porn. Pro-knowing the difference." The issue I'm tackling isn't porn, but instead it's the complete lack in our society of an open, healthy, honest, truthful dialogue around sex in the real world, which would then, among many other benefits, enable people to bring a real-world mind-set to the viewing of porn as artificial entertainment. Our message is simply "Talk about sex"—openly and honestly in the public sphere, and openly and honestly in your private, intimate relationships. Great sex is born out of great communication—all around.

I launched MakeLoveNotPorn with a talk at TED 2009,[4] and the response was extraordinary. The talk resonated with huge numbers of people globally—young and old, male and female, straight and gay, from every country in the world. They wrote and poured their hearts out to me. They told me things about their sex lives and their porn-watching habits that they had never told anyone else. You can read about this in detail in my short TED e-book, *Make Love Not Porn: Technology's Hardcore Impact on Human Behavior.*[5]

It was the cumulative impact of receiving those e-mails, day after day, that made me feel a personal responsibility to take MakeLoveNotPorn forward, in a way that would make it more far-reaching, helpful, and effective.

I decided to pursue our mission to "Talk about it" by deploying the dynamics of social media to socialize sex; to build a platform to act as sexual social currency, with the aim of making discussion around real-world sex more socially acceptable and socially shareable.

The Last Frontier of Video Sharing

I was lucky enough to be able to draw on the talents of an exceptional team to make this happen. My extremely talented cofounders on my first start-up, IfWeRanTheWorld, Corey Innis (CTO) and Oonie Chase (user experience lead), believed in MakeLoveNotPorn's mission so much that they wanted to cofound its next iteration with me. We hired our amazing community manager and curator, Sarah

Beall, and just over a year ago, we launched makelovenotporn.tv in open beta.

MakeLoveNotPorn.tv is MakeLoveNotPorn.com brought to life—a myth-busting, #realworldsex-celebrating, user-generated, crowd-sourced video-sharing platform, where anyone, from anywhere in the world, can submit videos of themselves having #realworldsex. My team and I curate—this is not YouPorn, PornHub, Xtube, where anyone can upload anything. We review every video before it's published. We operate a revenue-sharing business model: you pay to rent #realworldsex videos, and 50 percent of that income goes to our contributors, or as we like to call them, our MakeLoveNotPorn stars.

What Is #realworldsex?

MakeLoveNotPorn.tv is not porn. It's not amateur. It's #realworldsex.

What do we mean by that?

Well . . . #realworldsex is funny. If you can't laugh at yourselves when you're having sex, when can you? The same ridiculous shit happens to all of us—but we don't realize that because we don't share; it's more "OMG what happened last night was so excruciatingly embarrassing I can never talk about it to anyone ever!" Like, the nightmare of putting the condom on. In theory, it's one smooth seamless act; in practice, we all know it doesn't happen like that—and when it doesn't, things go soft, the moment passes, encounters get derailed. Queefing and fanny farts? Everyone does it. Nothing to be ashamed of. Hit us with the outtakes! Consider the appeal of "Charlie Bit My Finger"—at over five hundred million views on YouTube—and then consider the appeal of something as funny, spontaneous, and human in a sexual context. We want the sexual equivalent of *America's Funniest Home Videos* on MLNP.tv!

#realworldsex is messy. You think porn's dirty? Porn actually sanitizes sex. Nobody has hair. You never see anyone using lube, even though they go through gallons on set. You don't see any of those nice, fun, messy things that happen in the real world. So we welcome stuff like period sex. You don't see that in porn—and as a result, too many young men and women actually think you can't have sex during your period, even though that's when some women are at their horniest, and it's great!

#realworldsex is responsible. In porn, there are no condoms. Or if there are . . . suddenly the condom's on—Jump cut! Where did that come from? We want your hottest, most arousing #realworldsex videos actively competing to eroticize condom usage. What's the hottest way you can introduce a condom into the action? Put it on? Take it off? Dispose of it? I have sex with condoms all the time. I want to watch my kind of sex. Plus I want creative ideas for those awkward condom moments we all have. If more of us had more creative ideas on how to make using condoms hot and arousing, there'd be a lot more safe sex happening, a lot less disease transmission, and far fewer unwanted pregnancies. Between porn with no condoms and death-disease-and-disaster-prevention "roll the condom over the banana" classroom sex education, we see a gap in the market. We want to introduce a new sociocultural meme: #condomhot. MakeCondomhotLoveNotPorn—demonstrating not only that condoms don't get in the way of great sex but also that they can be an integral part of it. (Yes, there's a huge opportunity here for condom brands to partner with us, and yes, we're having a number of conversations about that.)

#realworldsex is lazy. You know that thing when you and your loved one have had a long, hard day? You're both lying in bed at the end of that long, hard day, totally knackered . . . but really horny? You want to get off, but you don't want to have to lift a finger to do it. Well, in the real world, that's when you have "sleepy sex" or "lazy person sex," which is what our community manager/curator Sarah Beall and her husband, Jon, call it. We want to showcase hot, creative ways to MakeLazyPersonLoveNotPorn, to prove you don't have to rock it like a porn star every time.

Socializing Sex

Think of all those celebrations of relationships that crop up in your Facebook timeline every day. Engagement announcements, wedding photos, lovey-dovey couple-y things . . . We're providing a platform to celebrate that last area of human relationships—the one that nobody else will let you share. The motivations, the dynamics, and the appeal are exactly the same. On Facebook, in your feed, your friends are sharing the fact that they're madly in love, on a romantic weekend in Paris, with photos of them kissing in front of the Eiffel Tower, eating in a cozy little French bistro, and strolling by the Seine. On MLNP.tv, your friends get to share the fact that they're madly in love, with a video of the amazing #realworldsex they had in their hotel room on that romantic weekend in Paris.

We have a particular design and copy philosophy for MLNP.tv. Apart from the actual videos themselves, everything on the site is safe for work. This is the site where, when somebody sits down next to you, unless you're actually streaming video, you never have to slam your laptop shut. We ensure that everything—copy, stills, thumbnails on videos—passes the test. You could be on an airplane (with Wi-Fi), laptop open at your seat to MLNP.tv; kids could be running up and down the aisle next to you, and as long as you're not playing video, it's perfectly fine.

We're currently in beta, real-world testing as we build, and further down the pipeline, we plan to include ratings, the ability to "follow" MakeLoveNotPorn stars, badges, stickers—all things that make it as open, easy, and fun to share #realworldsex as it is to share any other social content—but with our "social sex" mission at the heart of everything.

While we all have and enjoy sex, because we don't talk about it, we don't have a socially acceptable, socially shareable vocabulary for sex in the real world—one that everyone is comfortable using both in general, public discussions and for articulating how much you enjoy what goes on in your intimate relationships and what you'd like to do.

The language of porn has rushed in to fill that gap.

This isn't ideal, because, unsurprisingly given how male-dominated the management of the mainstream porn industry is, the language of porn is predominantly generated by men. The person who coined the term "fingerblasting" didn't have a vagina—because if you have a vagina, that term automatically makes you wince and want to cross your legs. The person who came up with the term "getting your ass railed" in straight porn, never had *his* ass railed. And while "bitch," "whore," and "slut" can be turn-ons in consensual dirty talk, to be addressed as such the very first time you get naked with someone can have quite the opposite effect. I'm speaking for myself and for the many people who've had similar experiences: the common male response when this approach is queried in a straight context is, "But women in porn really like it when you call them that." There are analogous "porn soundtrack" issues in gay and lesbian contexts.

We all feel vulnerable when we get naked. Quite often, we aren't sure what to say in bed or how to express ourselves verbally. We may have no other frame of reference other than porn for how people communicate during sex. Which can result in language and modes of address that are borrowed, inappropriate, and not necessarily welcome. Or, a reluctance to say anything at all—which is a shame, because talking and communicating during sex in whatever form you both (or all) enjoy is part of the fun.

So on MLNP.tv, we're creating a new vocabulary for #realworldsex. We don't tag our videos in the manner of the usual porn drop-down menu—"anal," "Asian," "hairy," "creampie," etc. We use terms like "juicy" and "succulent." Our term for "oral" is "downtown." We tag our anal-sex videos with a term based on the female experience of anal: "OwowowHEYNOW." We want to provide new language that you can use to talk about sex in public without worrying about being overheard and without feeling embarrassed about what's coming out of your mouth and that you can also use to talk about sex in private, in bed, to make it easier to ask for what you want in a gender-equal and positive way.

#realworldsex = #realworldconnection

What all of this means is that MLNP.tv plays a different role than porn does. We're not simply masturbatory material (although of course we are very happily that too). We are a fascinating glimpse into the raw, intimate sex lives of real people. Our core value proposition resides in the fact that everyone wants to know what everyone else is really doing in bed, but that nobody does know. Of all Internet porn billed as amateur, 99.99 percent isn't. (It's made by professionals masquerading as what people want to see.) The difference was articulated by one of our members, a man in his forties who has obviously watched a lot of porn, who told us, "When I watch your videos, I feel I've never seen people have sex before."

Another, younger, man summed up what we're all about perfectly when he said, "Watching porn makes me want to jerk off. Watching your videos makes me want to have sex." Like every other social media platform, we're about connecting people, through better understanding and communication, to help them get to better sex lives, to better relationships, to better lives, period.

We hear from our members all the time about how relationships, sex lives, and marriages have been rekindled by MLNP.tv, and we've even helped a couple who were trying to conceive. We're thrilled there's going to be a MakeLoveNotPorn baby![6]

The Battle We Fight

I had absolutely no idea when we embarked on this venture how extraordinarily difficult it was going to be to make it happen. It took me two years to get MLNP.tv funded. I should have been every angel investor's and venture capitalist's wet dream, literally. I was pitching an idea enabled by technology, designed to disrupt a sector worth billions of dollars, in a way that is both socially beneficial and potentially very lucrative. But because the sector is porn and the social benefit is to sexuality, no VC would touch it.

When I eventually found one angel investor who got it, and we closed on the seed funding we needed to build and launch the platform, I couldn't get my hands on the money for two months, because I couldn't find a single bank in America that would let me open a business bank account for a business that has the word "porn" in its name, and that does what we do.[7]

I still can't find a bank—anywhere in the world—that wants our business. Our biggest operational challenge has been putting a payment infrastructure in place. Because we're "adult content," PayPal and Amazon won't work with us; neither will mainstream payment and credit card processors.[8] And we have to explain to our bewildered members why we make it so hard for them to give us their money.[9] Business infrastructure that any other start-up can take for granted, we can't, because the small print always says, "No adult content."

I believe you can change the world through sex. My team and I are working to make sex better for all of us and to provide a healthy, real-world counterpoint to the ubiquitous influence of porn. The world of business and tech is doing everything it possibly can to stop us.

That's a very big mistake.

Lesson 1: Don't Care What Other People Think (in a Good Way)
Every obstacle to building our business that I've just described is driven by one dynamic and one dynamic alone: fear of what other people will think.

A young venture capitalist reached out to me last year—he'd seen me speak at a tech conference and was very interested in MakeLoveNotPorn. We met and talked. He totally got it, but he said to me, "At the end of the day, it's not about what I think. It's about what every other partner in my firm will think, and what every other investor in our fund will think."

Fear of what other people will think is the single most paralyzing dynamic in business, and in life.

As you've seen, I'm very open about the fact that I date younger men. That's because I would like to encourage more people to actively consider and design the relationship model that works for them—which may well be different at different stages of your life—versus the very limited number of relationship models society tells us it's OK to have. I'm equally open about the fact that I've never wanted to be married and I've never wanted children. I would like to see many more public role models celebrating the fact that you can live your life very differently from the traditional "marriage plus children" route that all of us are brought up believing is a given—and be very happy doing so.

I'm sharing the story of a start-up for which I have chosen a path that particularly requires me not to worry about what other people think. But this truth applies to everyone. The single best moment of my life, quite honestly, was when I realized I no longer gave a damn what anybody thought. It's the only way to live your life—being true to yourself, operating in line with your own beliefs and values. Try it at work. The next time you're in a meeting, speak up and say what you really think. Look around you, identify what you believe your company could do to better deliver against its business objectives, and put together and present a proposal to make that happen. Honesty and truthfulness pack a very powerful punch because we so rarely experience them in everyday and business life; everyone is too busy worrying what everyone else will think.

Step out of that trap, and you'll be amazed at the results.

Video-sharing #realworldsex Is Transformative

UK magazine *EasyLiving* published an article in its February 2013 issue by a woman who volunteered to make a #realworldsex video with her husband, submit it to us for publication, and write about the experience. She told us: "Making the film was one of the most rewarding experiences of my life and a fabulously bonding experience with my husband. I think you're really on to something." We were fascinated—we didn't realize when we started this venture that the actual process of making a #realworldsex video for MLNP.tv could in itself be relationship-transforming. Subsequently, we've heard from more and more of our MakeLoveNotPorn stars how rewarding the process of sharing their #realworldsex has been—particularly because when you decide to record yourselves having sex, you need to talk about it, and that dialogue has the potential to open up communication in a way that enables you to learn more about yourself, your partner, and your relationship. A couple from Mexico who go by the user name "Cato," said to us, "We thought we were open, but sharing our #realworldsex on MLNP.tv took our relationship to a whole new level."

Lesson 2: Everything in Life and in Business Is Improved by Better Communication

As you've seen, MakeLoveNotPorn was a complete accident. I never consciously planned or set out to do any of what I'm doing now—it was a result of coming across something I felt strongly about. But it's also the result of a career spent in the communications industry, and a strong sense therefore of the importance of great communication in everyday life and at work.

I believe one of the reasons the original MakeLoveNotPorn.com website has driven and continues to drive such an extraordinary response is because it is very simple, straightforward, honest, down-to-earth, utterly nonjudgmental, and it has a sense of humor. We rarely get to have conversations about sex within those parameters, and when we do, the floodgates open.

The same is true of everything else.

Deeply unhappy about something a friend has done? Reach out and talk about it. Having a difficult time with a coworker? Ask for a meeting in a private setting and put your concerns on the table calmly, straightforwardly, and honestly. Feeling your performance at work is not sufficiently valued? Schedule a conversation with your boss about it. Importantly, in a world of e-mail, instant messaging, chat, texting, skyping, always do this in person. It's astonishing how quickly you can straighten out misunderstandings face-to-face, when it's clear what everyone really means, and you are able to experience the nuances and true intentions that underlie any dialogue.

You get to better sex with better communication. You get to better everything with better communication. Our communication at MakeLoveNotPorn has drawn responses from some pretty surprising places.

What the Porn Industry Thinks

Among the thousands of responses I've received to MakeLoveNotPorn, there have been—much to my surprise when this first began happening—many responses from people in the porn industry. Specifically, Generation Y in porn—eighteen- to thirty-year-olds. Because Gen Y in porn is like Gen Y anywhere else: they're entrepreneurial and ambitious, questioning and challenging the old world order and wanting to be part of the new. Twentysomething porn stars and porn directors reached out to me of their own volition, telling me how much they loved MakeLoveNotPorn and that they wanted to help. As a result, we have a lot of friends in the porn industry supporting us—especially in our MLNP.tv category where we invite porn stars to share the sex they have off-camera, in the real world. Yes, porn stars have #realworldsex too, which is completely different from what they do in front of the camera. On MLNP. tv you can see young porn stars Danny Wylde and Lily LaBeau share the sex they had in their real-world relationship and explain in their intro video why they chose to do that.[10] Gay porn stars Dale Cooper and Colby Keller have posted their #realworldsex. Lesbian porn star Lily Cade shares the sex she has with her real-world girl-friends, many of whom also work in porn: they talk openly in their videos about how what they're doing differs from what they have to do on set. Porn star Aaliyah Love, romping around with Lily, says "I wish all porn could be like this." And retired porn star Kara Price says, "MLNP.tv may not be porn, but it's what porn should be."[11]

The porn industry generally is extremely supportive of and interested in what we are doing. Just two weeks after we first took MakeLoveNotPorn.tv live in private, closed beta in August of last year—tiny, bootstrapping, nobody could see what we were doing—we were on the home page of *XBIZ*, the porn industry's leading trade publication, with the headline "Cindy Gallop's New Website Takes Aim At Porn's Status Quo."[12] I give the porn industry full credit for seeing the disruptive potential of what we're doing well before the tech and business world—and *XBIZ* subsequently ran an in-depth interview with me in November 2012.[13]

We want MLNP to help the porn industry: to demonstrate that it is possible to invent a new, disruptive business model, and to leverage human sexuality as entertainment in a whole new way, in order to inspire the industry to create a better future for itself.

Our Business Model

Our business model is the opposite of the porn industry's. In porn, porn stars get paid by the scene. Payment for a scene will range from a few hundred dollars at the low end, to a thousand or so at the top end. That scene will go on to be viewed billions of times on Brazzers, Naughty America, and any number of tube sites, but the porn stars never see a cent from any of that. There are no residuals in porn. (If there were, every porn star would be a millionaire—nay, billionaire.) So porn stars have to supplement their income with selling their own clips, live camming, dancing, their own Fleshlight, if they're lucky—and, often, escort work.

Our model works the way the porn industry's should: the more people who enjoy your videos, the more you stand to make. I believe everyone should be rewarded for what they create. I feel particularly strongly about this because my background is in theater and advertising: two industries where ideas and creativity are massively undervalued, even by the creators themselves. Anyone who creates something that gives other people pleasure (in this case a *lot* of pleasure!) deserves to see a financial return. So half of what our members pay to rent each video—net a small amount to cover hosting, bandwidth, and transaction fees—goes to its creator(s), our MakeLoveNotPorn stars.

That's why we are the answer to the global economic crisis.[14]

MakeLoveNotPorn.tv is the Etsy of sexy. This is where you can make money from doing what comes naturally, the way it comes naturally. Never has the saying been truer: "Do what you love, and the money will come." And lots of other people will come too. It's a win-win!

We're thrilled when our members tell us they're happy to pay $5 to watch #realworldsex, because we're doing something nobody else is doing. And we're equally thrilled to hear how our MakeLoveNotPorn stars choose to spend their earnings, whether it's making a $500 donation to a charity they care about—Mr. and Mrs. Lau donated to Canines for Disabled Kids—or using the money for themselves, for doing good, or for investing back into the site by renting other MakeLoveNotPorn videos to support both them and us.

Where Disruption Is Needed like Nowhere Else

It's precisely because we now live in an unprecedented era of ubiquitous access to online porn, that we can't go on operating around sex and porn the way we always have—infused with shame and embarrassment, pretending neither exists. The solution isn't blocking, filtering, censoring—closing down. The solution is opening up.

The social solution is to "talk about it." We need everyone to rally round to instigate a seismic sociocultural shift to open up the conversation—in schools, with sex education that acknowledges the reality of porn, and across the nation, with tools, forums, and media that help parents talk openly to children and all of us talk openly to each other.

The business solution is to "disrupt it."

What nobody seems to realize in all the sensationalism and scaremongering going on around the influence of porn at the moment is that this is a business problem, that should be looked at through a business lens. No one's doing that, because the brilliant business minds that populate the management ranks of the Fortune 500, the pages of the *Harvard Business Review*, and the stages of conferences like TED have no interest in applying any of that brilliance to the adult industry.

They should.

Much that concerns people about porn is actually driven by its business problems as an industry. Porn has become so big, it has become conventional, with its own norms and rules—which is the reason much of it is so commodified and repetitive. It suffers from "collaborative competition," when everyone in a sector competes with everyone else in the sector by doing exactly the same thing everyone else in the sector is doing. And it's tanking. Its old world order business model has been destroyed by the advent of free porn online, and it hasn't invented a new model.

Everything I've cited is also true of music, television, publishing, journalism, and advertising. But in porn, those dynamics manifest in ways that are more controversial and distressing. The growth of extreme, violent porn is not the result of evil, twisted, malignant forces at work within the porn industry. Nor is it the result of an ever-more corrupted and depraved user base. It's the result, prosaically, of a bunch of business people terrified they're no longer making money, doing what business people in any sector terrified about not making money do: playing it safe. Looking at what everybody else is doing and then doing it too. The most obvious analogy is with another industry also suffering from collaborative competition—reality television, which originally disrupted TV with groundbreaking shows like *The Real World* and *The Osbournes*. Then everyone else jumped on the bandwagon, resulting in the current morass of ever-more voyeuristic, contrived, "how far can we push it" reality shows. As with reality TV, so with porn—especially when it's quick, easy, and cheap to churn out.

We almost all watch porn; we don't acknowledge it. Porn exists in a parallel universe, a shadowy otherworld. When you force anything into the shadows and underground, you make it a lot easier for bad things to happen, and a lot harder for good things to happen.

The answer is not to block porn, but to disrupt it.

The answer is to welcome, support, and fund entrepreneurs who want to disrupt and innovate, to change the world of sex and porn for the better. Encourage radical rethinking of business models; mentor, coach, advise, and help finance; establish tech incubators and accelerators for sex-related start-ups, or invite them into existing ones. Push to make business services open and available to adult ventures on the same basis and terms offered to everyone else. Provide support for those working on behalf of people in the adult industry to improve working conditions and treatment of talent, and to better business practices. Let's reinvent human sexuality as entertainment in innovative, healthier ways, and turn the future of sex and porn into something very different.

To paraphrase NRA president Wayne LaPierre's famous gun-debate quote, the only thing that stops a bad guy with a business is a good guy with a (better) business.

Silicon Valley encourages disruption and innovation in every other sector except this one—the one that needs it most. Silicon Valley, *this* is your Next Big Thing: the opportunity to disrupt the billion-dollar industry to end all billion-dollar industries.

Because, if nothing else will inspire VCs, angel investors, and tech thought leaders and influencers to act, ye gods, just think of the money to be made. In two areas, the second of which nobody ever considers, because nobody thinks it's possible. Obviously, there's money to be made out of sex—we all do it, we all enjoy it, it's recession-proof, the market never goes away. But consider the money to be made from socially acceptable sex. When you make sex socially acceptable and socially shareable, you potentially double, triple, even quadruple, the returns to be made on any investment in this area.

At the time of writing, MLNP.tv is just over a year old in public beta—a tiny, bootstrapping, underfunded start-up. We have over 250,000 members, growing month on month. We began generating revenue on day one, and have so far taken in revenue in the tens of thousands of dollars (in a world where the received wisdom is "nobody pays for porn," they're paying for #realworldsex). A number of our MakeLoveNotPorn stars are making four figures at each payout. We have gotten huge amounts of media coverage all around the world, without doing one single bit of media outreach ourselves. We are the globally recognized champions of real-world versus porn-world sex; some of our highest traffic sources are China, Indonesia, India, Pakistan—places where attitudes toward sex are most repressed. We are the universal call to action in this context: every day young people tweet "Make love not porn" on Twitter and each one thinks they thought of it first. Our marketing strategy is essentially one thing (but a very difficult thing to achieve): to be on page one of every single search engine's results for the word "porn." Currently we're result number thirty-five on page four of Google— not bad for a bootstrapping venture that has done no proactive search engine optimization.

In theory, with this amount of traction, we'd be perfectly positioned to raise a Series A round of funding. In practice, no one wants to know.

So we have to pave our own way. We have to break down societal barriers, not just generally, but in order to make our own business succeed.

Lesson 3: Make the Future of Money Work for You

I became so frustrated with the barriers we were facing, particularly on the payments front, that I said to Corey Innis, my cofounder and CTO, "We're trying to invent the future of porn; we want to find the people who are inventing the future of money. Let's find the people as frustrated as we are with the old world order of finance, money, payments—from a different perspective—because those are the guys that we want to work with." We researched the entire financial tech start-up landscape and identified the players we'd love to partner with—but then we discovered the new world order of money still subscribes to old world order legislation: the fine print still says "No adult content."

To reach the founders of those companies we wanted to work with, I tweeted at them—which is how we came to be working with Ben Milne of Dwolla, a PayPal challenger. When I pitched him MLNP.tv over Skype, there was silence, and then he said, "I don't know what to say, Cindy. I'm from Iowa." But he totally got it and supports our mission—as does Patrick Collison of Stripe, the gold standard for taking credit cards online. Unfortunately Patrick's bank doesn't, so Stripe can't work with us.

How is this relevant to you? I am now ferociously interested in the future of money. Every day I am checking on and exploring new payment start-ups, and I can tell you, the future of every industry is inextricably bound up with the future of payments in a way that I see very few people understanding.

Is the industry you work in in trouble? Are you wondering how on earth to make more money going forward? Do you want to start your own business? The future of payments enables you to redesign business models, to make payment seamless and invisible, to engage and transact simultaneously. If you want to revolutionize the way you do business, start seriously exploring the future of money.

This Is about All Our Futures

On September 26, 2013, Nancy Jo Sales published a *Vanity Fair* article subtitled "What Facebook, Twitter, Tinder, Instagram and Internet Porn Are Doing to America's Teenage Girls."[15] Its examination of the impact on young girls of pop culture that celebrates superficial sexualization, and the dating and social media apps that encourage that, drove a blogosphere maelstrom. Chris Sacca, a high-profile tech investor with a two-year-old daughter, tweeted his and his wife's concern: "@sacca This article has given @crystale and me nightmares. Actual nightmares."[16]

This isn't just about teenage girls, but also about teenage boys—who are also being socioculturally peer-pressured, into a particular construct of masculinity they can't escape.

What's interesting about the (admittedly sensationalized) article is that the various social networking applications cited are the products of a male-dominated tech world. Every one came from an all-male founding team, tech team, investor lineup, and advisory board. The net result is products born of a male worldview, of the type that the tech world loves.

Silicon Valley has been falling over itself to fund the problem. It's time to identify, support, and fund the solutions—many of which are now coming from women.

If you find what I and my team are doing with MakeLove-NotPorn intriguing and interesting, here's what I'd love you to take away from it: this is what a venture conceived by a woman, cofounded by two women and a man, and built by a tech team that is more female than male, looks like—genuinely innovative and disruptive.

Lesson 4: We Are the Innovators
We live in a world where the default setting is male. Men: you have no idea how much happier you would be living and working in a world that was fifty-fifty, equally designed and managed by women as well as men. None of us do. We've never lived in that world—yet.

We need to. Because diversity drives innovation. Many different perspectives, mind-sets, insights, and points of view coming together are what create true disruption. This is true of ethnicity, sexuality, and the area that cuts across them all: gender.

The day we have a porn industry that is equally informed, influenced, designed, driven, managed, and led by women as well as men, fifty-fifty; that targets 50 percent of its output at women as well as men; and that makes 50 percent of its money from women as well as men is the day we have a porn industry that looks very different. More creative, more innovative, more exciting, healthier, and more lucrative.

The same is true of every other industry.

Do you feel you have a different perspective from your male colleagues? That's what makes you valuable. Do you see that your male-dominated business isn't seizing the opportunities it could? Propose what it could be doing. Do you want to start your own business? Have the confidence to know you're going to be bringing something very different to the market.

Women challenge the status quo because we are never it. Which gives us a unique opportunity.

Designing the World We Want to Live In

As a tech entrepreneur, I read blogs, go to conferences, and engage in discussions that are about the impact of technology on humanity. With MakeLoveNotPorn, my team and I are tackling the single biggest impact that technology is currently having on the most fundamental aspect of humanity—our sexuality, which informs everything about how we feel about ourselves, other people, our relationships, our lives, our productivity, and our happiness. Our ultimate goal for MakeLoveNotPorn—a very ambitious one—is that one day, nobody will ever feel ashamed or embarrassed at having a naked photograph or a sex tape of themselves posted on the Internet—because it's simply a natural part of who we all are. When you take the shame and embarrassment out of sex, you defuse revenge porn—as well as many other things that have the potential to make human lives very unhappy.

That might sound like an impossible goal. But as the line from the Apple ad goes, "The people crazy enough to think they can change the world are the ones who do."

Lesson 5: Design Your Own Future—Because You Can

I believe the business model of the future is this: Shared Values + Shared Action = Shared Profit (financial profit and social profit). I designed MakeLoveNotPorn.tv around that business model, to be part of the collaborative economy—a new way of thinking about work and how you make money.

The old top-down economic model is broken—the model of making things happen through institutions, hierarchy, and organizations. There's a new bottom-up model emerging, of collaborative people-power and collective action. The collaborative economy isn't just the province of Uber, Airbnb, and TaskRabbit. It's the future of work.

In a world where job loss is due not only to the global financial meltdown and resultant recession worldwide but also to the increasing automation of labor and processes, MLNP.tv is an example of how people who share the same values can share something they all do, to benefit both society and themselves.

How would you like to design your own work in the collaborative economy? What do you most love doing? What are the conditions under which you most love doing it? How would you like to make money in that context? How can you leverage the future of money to help you design an opportunity, a job, a venture, a business model to deliver against all of that?

When you make open, honest communication your ally in everything you do; when you learn not to worry about what other people think; when you use financial innovation to come up with different ways of making money; when you wield diversity to disrupt; when you actively design your work, and your life, to be what you want it to be, you're making the world a better place, not just for you, but for everyone else as well.

Who wouldn't want that?

Notes

1. Tim Willingham, "The Stats on Internet Pornography," *Daily Infographic*, January 4, 2013, http://dailyinfographic.com/the-stats-on-internet-pornography-infographic.

2. "Kids Access Porn Sites at 6, Begin Flirting Online at 8," *USA Today*, May 14, 2013, http://www.usatoday.com/story/cybertruth/2013/05/14/childrens-online-safety-porn/2158015/.

3. Amy O'Leary, "So How Do We Talk About This? When Children See Internet Pornography," *New York Times*, May 9, 2012, http://www.nytimes.com/2012/05/10/garden/when-children-see-internet-pornography.html.

4. Matthew Trost, "Cindy Gallop: Make Love, Not Porn," *TED Blog*, December 2, 2009, http://blog.ted.com/2009/12/02/cindy_gallop_ma/.

5. Cindy Gallop, *Make Love Not Porn: Technology's Hardcore Impact on Human Behavior* (TED Books, 2011) Kindle edition.

6. "There's Going to Be a MakeLoveNotPornBaby!" *MLNP.tv* (blog), May 1, 2013, http://talkabout.makelovenotporn.tv/2013/05/01/theres-going-to-be-a-makelovenotpornbaby.

7. Daniel Wolfman and Chris Beier, "Too Sexy? 'No VC Wanted to Touch Me With a Barge Pole'," *Inc.*, September 13, 2012, http://www.inc.com/chris-beier-and-daniel-wolfman/venture-capital-cindy-gallop-make-love-not-porn.html.

8. Andrea Garcia-Vargas, "Why America's Outdated Morals Won't Let Porn into Mainstream Business," *Nerve*, July 10, 2013, http://www.nerve.com/features/why-americas-outdated-morals-wont-let-porn-into-mainstream-business.

9. Cindy Gallop, "Why We Make It So Hard for You to Give Us Your Money," *MLNP.tv* (blog), July 30, 2013, http://talkabout.makelovenotporn.tv/2013/07/30/why-we-make-it-so-hard-for-you-to-give-us-your-money/.

10. "Backstories Are Hot," *MLNP.tv* (blog), August 15, 2012, http://talkabout.makelovenotporn.tv/2012/08/15/contextisall/.

11. "Make Love Not Porn Might Not Be Porn, But It's What Porn Should Be / Kara Price," *MLNP.tv* (blog), August 7, 2013, http://talkabout.makelovenotporn.tv/2013/08/07/make-love-not-porn-might-not-be-porn-but-its-what-porn-should-be-kara-price/.

12. Bob Johnson, "Cindy Gallop's New Website Takes Aim at Porn's Status Quo," *XBIZ*, August 27, 2012, http://www.xbiz.com/news/153233.

13. Nelson Ayala, "Cindy Gallop Discusses MakeLoveNotPorn.tv," *XBIZ*, November 4, 2012, http://www.xbiz.com/news/156181.

14. Cindy Gallop, "How MakeLoveNotPorn.tv Can Help the Global Economy," *MLNP.tv* (blog), September 20, 2012, http://talkabout.makelovenotporn.tv/2012/09/20/how-makelovenotporn-tv-can-help-the-global-economy/.

15. Nancy Jo Sales, "Friends Without Benefits," *Vanity Fair*, September 26, 2013, http://www.vanityfair.com/culture/2013/09/social-media-internet-porn-teenage-girls.

16. Chris Sacca's Twitter account, September 30, 2013. https://twitter.com/sacca.

ACKNOWLEDGMENTS

Thank you to Katie Salisbury and Julia Cheiffetz at Amazon Publishing for helping conceptualize this collection and seeing it through to fruition.

Thank you to Lucy Carson at the Friedrich Agency for her sage advice throughout this process.

Thank you to Natalia Suárez for her terrific cover design (and for immediately understanding what we meant when we said "no heels, no cosmos, no italics").

Thank you to all our amazing contributors for being so enthusiastic about the project and for their willingness to share their stories (in no less than 5000 words!).

And finally, thank you to the group of women that is TheLi.st. We subscribe to the ideas that you can't be what you can't see and that there is a lot of money to be made by taking women seriously. Our goal with this collection was to showcase stories that demonstrate these theories in practice, and we're grateful to be surrounded by such a supportive group of successful, amazing women who daily embody both.

ABOUT TheLi.st

TheLi.st is a network and visibility platform for professional women from all industries who are ambitious, accomplished, and committed to helping each other rise. In 2013 it was named to *Forbes*'s 100 Best Websites for Women and *Business Insider*'s Silicon Alley 100, and it has been featured in the *New York Times*, *Marie Claire*, the *Guardian*, *Fast Company*, *Elle*, *BuzzFeed*, *Refinery29*, and more. Sign up for its regular newsletter at www.TheLi.st.

ABOUT THE EDITORS

 **Glynnis MacNicol** is a writer and cofounder of TheLi.st. Previously she was the media editor at *Business Insider* and a founding editor of *Mediaite*. She contributes to *Capital New York*. During the 2008 election year, she was a regular contributor to Playboy.com. Her work has also appeared in print and online for publications including *Marie Claire*, *The Daily Beast*, the *Huffington Post*, *Outside*, and *Maclean's*. She began her media career as an associate editor at the *Huffington Post* media blog *Eat the Press* and as the editor of *FishbowlNY*. Before that, she was a book publishing spy. Glynnis frequently speaks on the intersection of media and politics, and has appeared on CNN, Fox News, MSNBC, NBC, CBC, and Al Jazeera.

 **Rachel Sklar** is a writer and cofounder of TheLi.st. A former lawyer who writes about media, politics, culture, and technology, Sklar was a founding editor at the *Huffington Post* and *Mediaite* and has contributed to the *New York Times*, *Newsweek*, *The Daily Beast*,

HelloGiggles, *Elle*, *Glamour*, *Marie Claire*, *Politico*, and others. She is the author of *A Stroke of Luck: Life, Crisis and Rebirth of a Stroke Survivor* and has contributed to several anthologies, including *My Parents Were Awesome*, *Camp Camp: Where Fantasy Island Meets Lord of the Flies*, and *This Is Why You're Fat*. Rachel has been named to *Fast Company*'s League of Extraordinary Women, *Forbes*'s Women Changing the World, *Marie Claire*'s New Guard, *Business Insider*'s SA100, and has earned numerous honors and awards for her writing and her activism. Rachel speaks widely about media, diversity, politics, and culture; has appeared on CNN, Fox News, MSNBC, NBC, and CBC; and was a regular on *The Joy Behar Show* on HLN and Current.

ABOUT THE CONTRIBUTORS

Leslie Bradshaw is the chief operating officer of Guide, a Knight Foundation–backed technology company that leverages big data and visual storytelling to transform text to video for publishers. She also serves as a fellow at the US Chamber of Commerce, where she explores the economic and policy implications of big data, technology, and entrepreneurship. Having built a world-renowned data visualization company (JESS3) at the age of twenty-four—which during her tenure as president and COO counted Nike, Google, NASA, Samsung, C-SPAN, and Intel as clients, generated over $13 million in revenue, won *Ad Age* gold as the small agency of the year in the southeast region, and twice earned a spot on the Inc. 500 for revenues generated under her leadership—Leslie now sits on the advisory board of storytelling agency Beutler Ink and data visualization start-up Infoactive. For her contributions to the field of data visualization, Leslie has been recognized by *Fast Company* as one of "The Most Creative People in Business" and by *Inc.* magazine as a "Top 30 Entrepreneur Under 30." A Phi Beta Kappa graduate of The University of Chicago and cofounder of her family's pinot noir vineyard in Oregon's Willamette Valley, Leslie is also a regular contributor at *Forbes* on the topic of female entrepreneurship.

Nisha Chittal is a journalist and social media strategist who is the social media content editor for MSNBC. In this role, she develops social media strategy for the network's twenty-two show units, working closely with the show teams on editorial content, strategy, and campaign development. She also writes for MSNBC.com. Previously, Nisha led social media at Travel Channel in Washington, DC, and also worked at digital agency MXM Social, advising a variety of brands on social and digital strategy. Nisha has written about women's issues, politics, and technology for a variety of publications, including *Huffington Post, Poynter* online, *Ms.* magazine, *The American Prospect, Jezebel,* and others. She has also had essays published in two anthologies. She holds a bachelor's degree in political science from the University of Illinois at Urbana-Champaign.

Paula Froelich is the *New York Times* bestselling author of the novel *Mercury in Retrograde* and the nonfiction book *It! The Nine Secrets of the Rich and Famous That Will Take You to the Top.* She is best known in New York for being the deputy editor of the *New York Post's* gossip column, *Page Six,* where she worked for ten years until June 2009. She was also a correspondent for *Entertainment Tonight* and *The Insider* from 2002 to 2006 and has appeared as a guest on *The View, Real Time with Bill Maher, Today, Good Morning America, The Early Show, Entertainment Tonight, Extra, The Joy Behar Show,* and *The Howard Stern Show.* Before the *New York Post,* Paula was a financial reporter, covering interest rate swaps and over-the-counter derivatives for *Dow Jones Newswires* and *Institutional Investor*. She is currently a contributing editor for the Sundance Channel and *Playboy*, and freelances for the *New York Observer*, *Gourmet*, and *The Daily Beast*. In January 2012, she won a Gold Medal award from the North American Travel Journalists Association for her piece in *Playboy* on Iraq, "Down and Out in Baghdad."

 **Cindy Gallop** is a graduate of Somerville College, Oxford, whose background is brand-building, marketing, and advertising. She started up the US office of ad agency Bartle Bogle Hegarty in New York in 1998 and in 2003 was named Advertising Woman of the Year. She is the founder and CEO of www.IfWeRanTheWorld .com—co-action software that was launched in beta at TED 2010 and subsequently written up and taught as a Harvard Business School case study—and of www.makelovenotporn.com, launched at TED 2009. She and cofounders Corey Innis (CTO) and Oonie Chase (user experience lead) have just launched MakeLoveNotPorn .tv in public beta. She acts as board advisor to a number of tech ventures, sits on the Women at NBCU Advisory Board, and consults on brand and business innovation for companies around the world, describing her consultancy approach as, "I like to blow shit up. I am the Michael Bay of business." *Business Insider* last year named her one of 15 Most Important Marketing Strategy Thinkers Today, alongside Malcolm Gladwell and Seth Godin. She published *Make Love Not Porn: Technology's Hardcore Impact on Human Behavior* as one of TED's line of TED Books and is currently working on a book about her philosophy of life and business. You can follow her on Twitter @cindygallop.

Ruth Ann Harnisch is a writer, an investor, a coach, and a philanthropist. She is president of The Harnisch Foundation, which has given grants to hundreds of nonprofit organizations since its founding in 1998. She is a proponent of creative philanthropy whose unusual charitable investments have landed her on *Oprah* and the *Today* show. She is also an enthusiastic patron of the TED (Technology, Entertainment, Design) conference community, where she was a founding funder of the TED Fellows program. With Renee Freedman, she cocreated and codirects SupporTED, which provides free coaching and mentoring support to the TED Fellows. Ruth Ann is one of fewer than two hundred members of Women Moving Millions, who have given a minimum of a million dollar gift to causes that advance and empower women and girls.

Sally Kohn is one of the leading progressive voices in America. She is currently a CNN contributor and columnist for *The Daily Beast*. Sally was previously a Fox News contributor—the motivation for her widely seen TED talk—as well as a regular guest on MSNBC. Sally's writing has appeared in the *Washington Post*, *New York* magazine, *More* magazine, *Reuters*, *USA Today*, *Salon*, *Politico*, *Time*, and many other outlets. Her work has been highlighted by publications from the *New York Times* to *The Colbert Report* to the *National Review*, and Sally is ranked by *Mediaite* as one of the top one hundred most influential television pundits in America. Originally from Allentown, Pennsylvania, Sally now resides in Brooklyn, New York, with her partner, Sarah Hansen, and their daughter, Willa.

Since 2002, **Stacy London** has been best known as the straight-talking cohost on TLC's hit show *What Not to Wear*. Part psychologist, part style maven, Stacy utilizes her sassy sense of humor to not only help improve one's appearance on the outside but also help boost self-confidence from the inside. Starting her career in 1991 as an assistant at *Vogue* magazine, she quickly climbed the fashion ladder (in fabulous stilettos, of course!) and was appointed senior fashion editor at *Mademoiselle* from 1996 to 2000. She has styled runway shows for such designers as Rebecca Taylor and Vivienne Tam and has worked with celebrities such as Kate Winslet and Katie Holmes. She has served as brand ambassador and creative consultant for major companies such as Pantene, Lee Jeans, Woolite, Dr. Scholl's, and Westfield Shopping Malls. She is the author of the *New York Times* bestseller *The Truth about Style*, published by Viking. She has guest-hosted on the *Today* show (nine a.m. hour) and *The View*, and she can frequently be seen guest-hosting *Anderson Live*. Her highly anticipated jewelry collaboration with Sorrelli debuted in 2013. She lives in Brooklyn with her cat Baby Al, too many shoes, and not enough closet space.

Jenna Wortham is a technology reporter for the *New York Times*. She currently lives in Brooklyn.

Kindle Serials

This book was originally released in Episodes as a Kindle Serial. Kindle Serials launched in 2012 as a new way to experience serialized books. Kindle Serials allow readers to enjoy the story as the author creates it, purchasing once and receiving all existing Episodes immediately, followed by future Episodes as they are published. To find out more about Kindle Serials and to see the current selection of Serials titles, visit www.amazon.com/kindleserials.